"Exploring ancestral patterns can be a painful journey, especially when the road is paved with skeletons that haunt us along the way. Thankfully, Nancy Hendrickson's valuable book brims with techniques for uncovering where our ancestral inheritances may have originated and why we sometimes feel the impulse to act them out. Each exercise magically transforms the ancestral agenda, becoming a curative lesson in freeing ourselves from repeating outdated stories. *Ancestral Tarot* is a sound ally and advocate for healing the generational wound." —Carrie Paris, creator of *The Relative Tarot*

"A powerful, revelatory guidebook on using tarot to connect with your ancestors, Hendrickson's *Ancestral Tarot* meets you where you are on your spiritual journey and takes you farther, opening you up to an expansive world of psychic insight. Learn how to unveil long forgotten ancestral memories and cultivate stronger bonds with your spirit guides. Hendrickson is an authoritative voice I trust." —Benebell Wen, author of *Holistic Tarot*

"Wisdom and insights from those whom we have inherited our diverse cultures and customs are revealed through Nancy Hendrickson's accessible tarot-reading techniques. *Ancestral Tarot* will prove to be a go-to resource for tarot practitioners." —Gina G. Thies, author and creator of *Tarot of the Moors*

"Hendrickson magnificently breaks new ground with *Ancestral Tarot*. There has never been a tarot book like this, and we have never needed a book like this as much as we do now. In warm, accessible prose, she opens exciting new possibilities for using tarot to explore ancestral connection. A must-have on any serious tarot bookshelf, offering deep, important exercises for personal growth and divinatory practice!" —Thalassa, creatrix of the San Francisco Bay Area Tarot Symposium and founder of Daughters of Divination

"*Ancestral Tarot* gives us practical tools and spiritual guidance to use tarot for personal healing and exploration in a way that is deep, meaningful, and masterful." —Christiana Gaudet, author of *Tarot Tour Guide* and *Fortune Stellar*

"Bravo! Nancy leaves *no* stone unturned in her phenomenal tarot debut! Working through her spreads helped me connect to one of my ancestors almost immediately and I have been growing the connection ever since. She takes a very intangible practice and makes it practical, hands-on, and very down to earth. If you seek to facilitate a connection to a loved one or do the work to recognize and break generational patterns, this book is for you!" —V. of RedLight Readings, the Tarot BFF

"*Ancestral Tarot* takes what can be a very daunting, complex topic and creates a simplified way to learn and experience your ancestors. The journal pages and tarot spreads led me on an unexpected journey. I especially enjoyed the methods of making and using sigils. Hendrickson offers a variety of tools to help you connect and work with the people in your past." —Debbie Chapnick, author of the *Tarot Tip Sheet* and *The Journey of the Food*

"*Ancestral Tarot* is a level up when it comes to ancestral work and divination. Hendrickson has created a pathway with guardrails for each reader to follow along their journey. A work of self-discovery, this book invites us to travel back in time to connect with ancestral history and forward to know how our work today prepares us for our future role as ancestor. The spreads, writing prompts, and exercises included are accessible to both new and experienced readers. When you're ready, grab your cards, a pen and journal, and turn the page to chapter 1." —Rhonda Alin, founder of Northern New Jersey Tarot Study Group

"*Ancestral Tarot* will enable people with disrupted or strained family backstories to heal that rift. Very hands-on and with deep foundations in Nancy's own ancestral practice and excellent tarot skills. Nancy is a born teacher!" —Alison Cross, author of *A Year in the Wildwood* and *Tarot Kaizen*

"Nancy Hendrickson repurposes the art of tarot to manifest a divinatory window to the past. *Ancestral Tarot* provides a unique and in-depth way to examine the family tree, untangle complicated histories, facilitate healing, and adjust the lineage onto a positive path for the future. If you are a genealogy buff who would enjoy a new way of interacting with the Ancestors, this book should be on your shelf." —Cairelle Crow, genealogist and founder of *Sacred Roots Genealogy*

"*Ancestral Tarot* asks all the right questions to connect with our ancestors, so that we can gain wisdom. The book's many layouts help us to see family patterns with the detail and nuance we need. Healing relationships with our ancestral patterns not only heals us, it reaches forward into future generations enabling us to become what this changing world needs—wise and whole. A 'must have' book!" —Jessica Macbeth, author of *The Faeries' Oracle*

ANCESTRAL
T·A·R·O·T

*Uncover Your Past
and Chart Your Future*

NANCY HENDRICKSON

foreword by Theresa Reed, The Tarot Lady

**WEISER
BOOKS**

To family, of course

This edition first published in 2021 by Weiser Books, an imprint of
Red Wheel/Weiser, LLC
With offices at:
65 Parker Street, Suite 7
Newburyport, MA 01950
www.redwheelweiser.com

ISBN: 978-1-57863-741-6
Library of Congress Cataloging-in-Publication Data available upon request.

Cover and text design by Kathryn Sky-Peck
Interior photos/images from the *Rider-Waite-Smith Tarot*
Typeset in ITC Berkeley Oldstyle

Printed in Canada
MAR
10 9 8 7 6 5 4 3 2

Table of Contents

Acknowledgments

So many people to thank, so much gratitude to offer.

First, to Fred West, John Hijatt, and Patti Testerman, all supreme supporters of the book and of me, thank you for reminding me that patience is a virtue.

A big thanks, as well, to the members of the San Diego Tarot Collective. I'd also like to send out special thanks to my Instagram friends, especially Kate Majeski, who graciously tried out my very first Ancestral Tarot spread. And, to Becca Gray, whose reading helped me recover the X factor I knew was missing from the book—me.

This project went through multiple iterations, as books tend to do. Fortunately, I had many discussions along the way that helped solidify my ideas. Thank you to all who listened. My gratitude to Theresa Reed for her wise counsel and to Joanna Powell Colbert for lighting the spark that would become this book.

I'm not sure any of this would have been written had it not been for the many years of deeply personal and insightful dialogues with *Faeries' Oracle* author Jessica Macbeth. I'm convinced she holds the knowledge of all things.

Finally, a huge thanks to Judika Illes, the editor who supported my idea from the very beginning. She gave me guidance, feedback, and an ongoing belief in the project. Her confidence fueled the book—and me—from start to finish. I suspect the ancestors had a hand in guiding me to her—how else could it have been such a perfect fit.

Foreword

I never paid much attention to my ancestors. Frankly, I didn't feel connected to my family of origin. Part of me was secretly convinced that I was adopted and belonged to some bohemian intellectuals instead of the simple farm folk that were my kin. But my father's blue eyes and violent temper were clear markers that I did indeed belong to this family, and I could not deny my heritage.

Although there were a few family stories I recall fondly, most of the tales in our tree were about drinking, violence, and loss. Is it any wonder that I wanted to get as far away from that energy as possible? I didn't want any part of it. Why bother knowing more when what you knew wasn't happy?

A few years ago, my daughter started playing around with genealogy, the study of family history. She is a writer of historical fiction, so this was something she was keenly interested in. I also suspect she wanted to know more about our lineage, especially since I didn't have too much to say about it other than my own negative perceptions.

Soon, she was reporting back with stories of ancestors who were writers, preachers, and warriors with names like Experience Wing and Dudley Tyng. One of our relatives was a rabble-rousing anarchist who tried to take on the post office. Others came over on the *Mayflower,* among the first Europeans to land in America. Eventually she traced our lineage all the way back to Charlemagne, the emperor from the Middle Ages. This got my attention.

Suddenly, I yearned to connect with my history. I wanted new stories about the people from my past, a deeper understanding of what went wrong along the way . . . and perhaps a way to fix it. Since my parents were long gone, and most of my elderly relatives had passed on as well, that seemed like an impossible dream.

Then *Ancestral Tarot* from Nancy Hendrickson landed in my lap—and everything came together. Even though I had been reading tarot for over forty years, never once did I consider using the cards to uncover the past. I've always been "future-oriented" and looking for ways to prevent problems. But what if I could go back to the root? Could I break the wheel and create change for future generations? I started with that thought and began to work my way through the exercises in this book.

Starting with the Journey Spread, *Ancestral Tarot* takes you down a winding path that will allow you to see your heritage with new eyes. You'll learn about the different types of ancestors, including the Ancestors of Blood, Place, and Time, and pick a Spirit Guide. (I chose my Aunt Deal, who baked my favorite cakes and cookies.) Next, you'll learn about omens, dreams, prayer, and rituals. Different methods of choosing cards for the deceased give clues to the family patterns and dynamics that have been in place long before you were born.

The tarot spreads in the book help to unravel karmic debts and heal the hidden wounds that may have been impacting your life on a subconscious level. If you've ever wondered why the members of your family—and you—sometimes do certain things for "no reason" that can be explained, the exercises in *Ancestral Tarot* will help you see exactly what started that familial pattern.

Laying out a family tree based on Nancy's methods was the most impactful part of the book. Suddenly, I could see how I was more like my family than I had thought. The Family Pattern Spread provided insights to begin healing those parts I didn't like in them . . . or myself. Spreads for past lives, inner child work, and mandalas opened me up in surprising ways. Suddenly, I was feeling good about my bloodline . . . and the new pathways I've created for my own offspring.

Ancestral Tarot is unlike any tarot book I've ever worked with before. It had a profound effect on the way I feel about my family and myself. Nancy's exercises, spreads, prompts, and suggestions have created a rich body of work that will change generations, as well as our understanding of the past.

Nancy states in the intro: "Using my cards, I've resolved family issues that were once ignored, found comfort when my mother passed over, and experienced healing from a wound I didn't even know existed."

I can say that this has been my experience too, using the methods in *Ancestral Tarot*. This is a book whose time has come and is sure to be a well-used resource for both tarot fans and students of genealogy.

When you tend to the roots of your past, the future of your family can flourish like never before.

Blessings,
Theresa Reed, author of
Tarot: No Questions Asked—Mastering the Art of Intuitive Reading

Introduction

I've spent a lifetime chasing dead people. I suppose that's because death came early to the family. When I was one, my grandfather left the planet. At age three we lost my week-old brother, at twelve my grandmother, at fifteen my dad, and, a year later, a cousin. Death seemed to be an unwanted guest that we couldn't get out the door.

How could I not have an interest in the Great Beyond when I knew so many people who lived there?

Looking back, I realize that even at a young age, I knew—somehow—that the ancestors were part of a special tribe to which I belonged. As it turns out, I wasn't the only person in the family who was interested in the afterlife. As an adult, I discovered that my grandparents had attended séances during which messages were received from long-gone family. How improbable, in afterthought, that their connection to Spirit was kept secret for so long.

Growing up, I was always drawn to the past, not only because of my early experiences with death, but because both grandmothers filled my head with stories about covered wagons and Civil War raiders. For me, traveling back in time to see long-gone ancestors was as normal as meeting friends for coffee. It is any wonder that I've devoted years to writing countless books and magazine articles about the ancestors?

The older I got and the more paranormal experiences I had, the more I knew without a doubt that another world existed beyond my own. Call it what you will, but I know with certainty that there is a time or an energy beyond our easily visible one. That other place, the one that's right along-side us and sometimes within us, is where the ancestors dwell. That's the world I've been able to touch most of my life, and it's the world I want you to experience firsthand.

When you learn about your ancestors, you'll gain a strength that's inde-scribable. While you may have had hard times with some family when they were still alive, you have millions more in Spirit who are cheering you on. There really is a magic in this work.

Part of that magic is that you never know what you're going to discover. Even as I was writing this book, testing spreads, and working out how best to download my brain to yours, I was constantly surprised. The messages from beyond were so simple and yet so powerful.

On one occasion, I was testing a spread, trying to understand why one of my grandmothers and I had had such a difficult relationship. While pulling cards I had a sudden memory flash. When I was very young, I developed a growth on one of my wrists that was scheduled to be excised. Grandma told me that if I wiped the growth with a used dishcloth, then buried the cloth under the light of the moon, the growth would disap-pear. I can still see her wiping my wrist, then walking up behind the garage to bury the cloth. The next day, the growth was gone. As I looked back on that incident, I realized that she was practicing a very old form of folk magic.

I learned, thanks to my sister, that almost everything Grandma did was timed to a specific phase of the moon. That's probably why her vegetable garden flourished. Who would have thought that all those memories would emerge thanks to tarot? That spread alone helped me understand her more than I ever did while she lived.

Over the years, I have discovered that ancestral work is multifaceted. You're going to run into ancestors who are so excited to work with you that they practically jump off the cards. You'll also find those who don't want to be involved at all. There, too, are those who created family patterns that destroyed generations. And, of course, you'll find the ancestors you loved so much that touching in with them can begin to heal even the most broken of hearts.

I realize that doing Ancestral Tarot can trigger old memories—including hurtful experiences as well as loving remembrances. Ancestors—especially the ones you knew—can be the source of incredible pain or incredible love. You'll be working with both throughout this book. And if an exercise brings up stuff you don't want to deal with today, don't hesitate to step back. We all work through issues in our own time. The choice is always yours to make.

As you read through the chapters, with your tarot cards and journal at hand, one thing I do want to ask is that you be open to the messages you receive. Your ancestors were real people with dreams as precious as your own, and in general, they like communicating with you. While their messages may sometimes feel as if they are coming out of left field, for the most part the ancestors are doing their best to guide, protect, encourage, heal, and love you. What's up to you is being open enough to recognize when you're getting a message and having the willingness to listen to it.

I guarantee there will be days when you'll shake your head at what you're hearing, wondering if it's just some fantasy created for your own amusement. When one of my ancestors told me that I'd be writing seven more books after this one, I have to admit I thought he was crazy. On this message—just like some you'll receive—only time will tell. But while we work together, let's agree that whatever pops into your head, or whatever you "see" or "hear," is exactly the message you're meant to receive—however wacky it might sound.

Ancestral work is sacred to me, and I hope through this book it becomes sacred to you. I understand you may find this to be a ridiculous statement if your family experience has been a nightmare. If that's so, then my heart goes out to you. I believe you'll feel differently as you work back past the generations and discover the ancestors that cherish you.

As I was putting this book together, I thought about the many ways people communicate with Spirit. Some become mediums, while others depend on dreams or omens. For me, tarot is the treasure map. Using my cards, I've resolved family issues that were once ignored, found comfort when my mother passed over, and experienced healing from a wound I didn't even know existed.

I hope this book does the same for you.

There's one last thing about ancestral work that I want you know. I have turned over every leaf possible to find my family. But in the end, what I came to realize is that the search for ancestors is really about a search for self. Work with the ancestors and the person you'll find is *you*.

So grab a journal, a couple of tarot decks, a great hunk of curiosity, and turn the page.

The Journey Spread

You can't start a tarot book without a spread, right? Before reading further, get out your tarot deck, shuffle, and do this spread. Keep notes in your journal about which cards you drew and your impressions. Then, be sure to come back to these notes when you've finished the book to compare how the ancestral work you have done corresponds to the cards you draw today. Happy Journey!

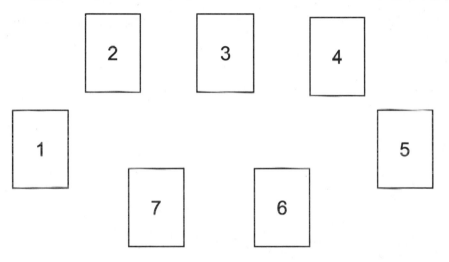

Card 1. Me, today

Card 2. The bridge I'll be crossing to meet the ancestors

Card 3. What do the ancestors think of me?

Card 4. What do I think of the ancestors?

Card 5. What is the goal of my journey?

Card 6. The unexpected

Card 7. How will Ancestral Tarot affect my life?

How to Use This Book

There is no particular order required for you to read this book. If working with issues from your family of origin is most important to you, you may want to start with chapter 5. However, I encourage you to begin at the beginning and explore the many tarot spreads and Journal Prompts before doing a deep dive into long-standing family issues.

Chapters 1–3 will briefly introduce you to the three major types of ancestors: Ancestors of Blood, Place, and Time. Once you have a basic understanding of these groups, you'll pull cards to decide which type of ancestor is best for you to begin working with right now.

You'll also find a chapter on meeting and working with a Spirit Guide, as well as creating a team of spirit helpers. Chapter 3 will load you up with a variety of tools for the journey. I hope your backpack is supersized—because you'll be given a lot to work with!

In chapter 4 the journey begins by working with your present family. You'll discover how to correlate tarot cards with family members and compare them with your own cards. This is where you'll begin to see family patterns forming.

Chapters 5, 6, and 7 do a deep dive into the three ancestral types. These are the chapters that dig into the nitty-gritty of family patterns, healing, past lives, adoption, and DNA. Chapter 8 covers the ins and outs of keeping a daily tarot journal if you're not already doing it.

Chapters 9–11 will put a bow on all that you've learned by introducing you to a world of ancestral altars, sacred space, and crystal grids. Chapter 9 breaks some exciting new ground around life-and-death concepts. Chapter 10 will walk you through creating a Whole Self Mandala. Bonus points for doing more than one mandala and then comparing them side by side with your own. I guarantee at least one surprise.

Sprinkled throughout are Sacred Tools that I hope you'll incorporate into your Ancestral Tarot process.

If you want to learn more about the topics discussed, see the appendices for some Tarot 101, suggested supplemental reading, and free genealogy resources.

Chapter 1

Beyond the Veil

There are more things in heaven and Earth, Horatio,
Than are dreamt of in your philosophy.
—HAMLET

In the last few weeks of my mom's life she saw her long-deceased mother by her side. "Mom's standing next to me," she would say.

Mom's vision was a common one; it's been well-documented that when people are close to death they see or converse with relatives who have already crossed over. But those close-to-death experiences are far from the only time we experience ancestral communications.

There is an undeniable energy that is ongoing and familial. For me—and for millions living from one end of the spiritual spectrum to the other—there's a certainty that the essence of our ancestors lives on, probably forever. And while we, using tarot, want to communicate with our ancestors, the truth is, they're already communicating with us. If you're tuned in, you know this. You may hear whispers during meditation or interact with long-gone family in your dreams, or like me, actually see spirits who are trying to get your attention. But if all this is new to you, hang on 'cause I'm going to show you how to begin listening.

WHO ARE THE ANCESTORS?

But first, exactly who *are* the ancestors?

When we think about an ancestor, the immediate image is of our own blood lineage, e.g., great-great-uncles, 10x great-grandfathers . . . you know, the whole family tree. But based on the culture you come from or relate to, an ancestor may differ from a "dead person," based on how recent or distant their passing.

I'm all for keeping things simple, and this book isn't intended to be a comparative religion guide to the afterworld. For our purposes, I'm referring to ancestors as people who are now in Spirit. This means they may have passed over last month or hundreds of years ago.

I work with three different types of ancestors. Let's meet them now.

ANCESTORS COME IN ALL FLAVORS

Ancestors of Blood

Ancestors of Blood are those with whom you share genetic material. Some ancestors you knew during their lifetime; most you did not. Ancestors of Blood will probably be the largest group of people with whom you'll work. That's because family is like a seesaw—one day offering you happiness, and the next, grief.

When you think of genetic ancestors, you know that their DNA runs through you just as surely as their blood flows in your veins. You share not only their physical traits but also their emotional profiles and behaviors.

These ancestors' genetic or ancestral memories are hardwired into your system; let's call it your *genetic inheritance*. The Ancestors of Blood are the ones from whom—via either nature or nurture—you've inherited family patterns that have taught you how to navigate the world. Sadly, some of those patterns won't guide you to the X on the treasure map. Instead, they'll run your ship aground on some deserted island. Fortunately, you'll learn how to deal with those issues later in this book.

The Ancestors of Blood we can relate to most immediately—and probably the ones we most want to work with—fall into two categories: those you want to honor and those who inflicted wounds that sorely need healing. And in case you're wondering—no, you never have to honor an ancestor who made your life a living hell, but it's my prayer that you take the first steps toward healing *you*.

Your blood ancestors come down two lines: one from your dad (paternal) and one from your mom (maternal). *Direct* blood ancestors are those in a straight line from someone down to you. In other words, your dad's dad's dad or your mom's mom's mom.

Now where this whole blood ancestor thing can get tricky is when, somewhere along the line, the "father" listed on a document wasn't the real father. This happens more often than you might think, which is one of the reasons DNA has become such a popular tool for finding "real" ancestors (chapter 6).

But, false fatherhoods aside, when I refer to Ancestors of Blood, I'm talking about the people along your family line who created you.

Without taking a deep dive into history, just let me also say that all your ancestors go back to the beginning of humans on Earth. According to the brainiacs, we all came out of Africa, then spread across the globe. There was a great book published several years ago called *The Seven Daughters of Eve* in which DNA expert Bryan Sykes takes us back to those he calls the seven original Eves—the mothers of us all. You'll meet those early, original ancestors in chapter 5. Although they lived so long ago that we can hardly wrap our heads around it, they are still blood ancestors.

Note: Modern humans as we know them were not the only human-like species running around populating the world. It's been well-documented that modern humans interbred with other species including Neanderthals and Denisovans. Some DNA companies can tell you if you have some tiny percentage of Neanderthal DNA. (Yes, for the record, I do.)

Ancestors of Those Who Were Adopted

If you were adopted, you may feel as though you have no ancestors. That's not true. You have just as many as anyone else even though you may know less about them. My hope, if your parentage is unknown, is that one day you will find a DNA match that will lead to your blood family. That, then, will lead you to your own precious lineage.

If you want to discover your blood family, my best advice is to persevere. More and more adoption records are opening, and my wish is that one of them is yours. The second thing I'd tell you if you were sitting across from me now is that I personally have found parental lineage via DNA, so it's not so outlandish that the same thing could happen to you.

At age ninety, my mother found her father. And just in the last year, through DNA, I was able to find the biological parents of a Jewish adoptee, even though the birth parents were born in Romania and lived in the Jewish ghettos of both Chicago and New York. Blood will out. They will be found.

If you're adopted, you can still do every exercise in this book. *Although you may never know your blood ancestors, trust me, they know you.* Your intent will guide them to you just as surely as the lamp of the tarot's Hermit sends rays into darkness.

Ancestors of Place

If you are a Native American or live outside North America, you may already know the customs and cultures of your family's place of origin. But if your family immigrated to the Colonies or later to what became the United States or Canada, clues about your ethnic origins may only come from family stories, legends, or lore. Or they may be totally lost in time.

While the Ancestors of Place have a genetic connection, you may never have heard of them or had any awareness of their existence. They could have lived far beyond your recent memory, originating in a place you never knew as home.

Maybe you heard a family story about your Ancestors of Place coming from the "Old Country." Unfortunately, that story isn't as helpful as knowing they originated in Ireland or came to North America because their Quaker-ism bought them a ticket to an English prison. Hopefully, your tarot work will open more of those detailed doors.

For our purposes, Ancestors of Place are relatives who lived in your family's places of origin. If you've traveled extensively and stayed in a town where you felt right at home, I'm betting that you unknowingly stumbled upon a place of origin.

There's one more thing. In this group, I also include the spirits that our distant ancestors probably knew well, but have become lost in our modern histories. Our long-ago ancestors were so connected to nature that they knew a whole host of beings outside our experience. Among them are entities like the Aos Sí, tree spirits, the goddess of the moon, and the Thunderbirds.

Ancestors of Time

I have no idea how many lifetimes we have all lived. But I do know that we've lived them. There are places and people we are so drawn to that it's clear we knew them in another incarnation. Ancestors of Time are those from past incarnations.

My sister Vicki connects to the washerwomen who worked at Fort Laramie, Wyoming, in the 1800s. For Patti, Ireland is where she feels the most at home. John felt a sense of peace and magic while sitting by the shore on the Aran island of Inishmore. He is drawn to runes and Nordic lore as fervently as Vicki is to laundry.

As for myself, I've tapped into many lifetimes. Whenever I visit the Little Bighorn Battlefield, I have an incredible sense of joy because it feels like I'm connecting with old friends. I'm also drawn to World War I biplanes and the Ancestral Puebloan (Anasazi) ruins that are strewn across the Southwest. Standing on the ramparts of Stirling Castle in Scotland, I felt I had come home.

Many lives, many memories.

Ancestors of Time include those people and family from another of your incarnations. For me, connecting with them can be just as important as connecting with Ancestors of Blood because I know that those other lifetimes impact me today. I want to understand how past patterns have stayed with me through many incarnations—and how to embrace them, heal them, or let them go.

Included in this group of ancestors are people who could have nongenetic connections to you in this lifetime. Or, who knows, your parents today may have been your siblings in another life.

The Ancestors Are Closer Than You Think

You may not realize it, but you receive ancestral messages all the time. Although this book focuses on using tarot for ancestor work, there are many ways our ancestors communicate with us. Once you recognize and open those portals, tarot will enhance them tenfold.

Smell

When one of my uncles crossed over, my mom—his sister—asked that he let her know he was okay. That night she smelled his aftershave. Similarly, she had periods of time when the scent of her mother's perfume filled her apartment.

If you've smelled a fragrance from someone who has passed over, they're letting you know that they're close to you. As in my mom's situation, the fragrance may be an aftershave, or it could be roses, lily of the valley, or cigarette smoke. We pick up on those fragrances as a reminder that someone we loved is with us. They want to let us know they're around.

Feathers

I don't know about where you live, but where I am, seeing feathers is not all that common. So for me, feathers are like little blessings dropped in front of me from the ancestors. You may ask, "So what? It's just a feather."

Not really.

We're getting messages all the time, but we frequently pass them off as coincidences or things with no greater meaning than "it's just a feather."

To communicate with the ancestors, you'll need to be receptive and begin asking questions. You're going to get plenty of practice with tarot, but why not request a message the next time you see a feather? And there's always a message. It may not always be from the ancestors, but when you chance upon a feather, someone's trying to get your attention.

Waking Up at the Same Time Nightly

Before my mom passed away, she told me that after she was gone, she would communicate by coming to me in the night. And do you know what? I wake up almost every night at 2:00 a.m. I remember telling her that it might interrupt my sleep, but that didn't seem to faze her.

If your ancestor is waking you up at the same time nightly, maybe it's because they can't get your attention any other way. Ancestor alarm clocks, anyone?

Significant Events

My sister's Christmas tree has always had non-blinking lights. But for two years running, each Christmas Eve—and only on Christmas Eve—all the lights on her tree started to blink and did so all evening. She's convinced that it was our stepfather just stopping by to say hello.

Other ancestors have communicated by making lights flicker or by turning electrical appliances like the TV on and off.

In my experience, these electrical messages tend to come shortly after a death or during an emotionally turbulent time. One family member finally had to unplug her television one night because it turned itself on and off four different times. Not a surprise as she was in a time of crisis and major stress. Who was there, trying to assure her that she was being watched over?

Music

I've had music communications from my mother on three separate occasions. I think it's when she knows I need her most.

After my mom's memorial service in July, I was driving home, and my phone started playing a Christmas song that was stored in the cloud. That in itself was startling enough, but the lyrics included the line: "How do you measure the love of a mother?" There was no doubt in my mind that Mom was letting me know she was okay, but more than that, she wanted me to know that she was with me.

The other two times happened after I took flowers to the cemetery. On both occasions, on heading home, my phone pulled another song from the cloud: the Hallelujah Chorus from Handel's *Messiah*—one of Mom's favorites.

There is zero doubt in my mind that my mother was there—reaching out to me when she knew I was struggling with the loss.

Repeating Numbers

Who hasn't seen 4:44 or 3:33 on a clock? Some people refer to these repeating numbers as angel numbers. Are the ancestors really angels? I'll have to defer that question to someone who knows far more about angels than I do.

I tend to see 1:11 or 11:11 most often. Because I started life as a numerologist, I know that 11 and 22 are both master numbers, so I do try to pay attention to what's going on when I see them. If you spot repeating numbers, they may be a loved one's birthday or an anniversary or a code the two of you decided upon prior to your loved one's passing.

Dreams

My most vivid example of a dream visitation came a few years ago. A friend had suddenly passed over. The night of his passing I had an unforgettable dream in which he called me on the phone saying, "I've been trying to call Mary [his wife] but she won't pick up. Would you call and tell her that I'm fine?"

Although Mary was psychic, she was so distraught she couldn't get grounded enough to receive his message. I became the go-between.

In yet another instance, I had written a petition asking for a message from the ancestors. That night I dreamed that I opened a door and standing there was one of my grandmothers. Behind her was her mother and her mother and her mother—an endless line of the women who came before me. The dream was life-affirming and a clear message of how supported I am.

What Messages Do You Think You're Already Receiving?

As you read through the various methods of ancestor communication, do any of them seem familiar? If any of these types of messages have happened to you, congratulations. The ancestors are already working with you.

In whatever way your messages are coming through, write down what you were doing at the time or how you were thinking or feeling. Maybe you're one of those who get messages when you're feeling down. Or maybe messages come at a time when you need to make an important decision. A message received on the day of an ancestor's passing can have a special meaning just for you.

Although I walk daily, I can't say that I love every walk I take. But on the days when a feather floats into my path or I hear words coming from a beautiful flower, I know I'm being supported by an ancestor in spirit who wants me to know how good it is for me to keep up this habit. Not only does it feed my soul, but it strengthens my body, clears my mind, and helps me let go of anything that's really bugging me.

You may feel the same way if a hummingbird buzzes your head or a ladybug lands on your hand. If nature isn't your thing, my guess is your ancestor or ancestors may get your attention by that tricky little electrical on-off thing they do.

If you've already noticed these kinds of messages, take a time-out and drop a few words into your journal. I don't want you to forget them. Two to three chapters down the road, you may not clearly remember the message you received today. Write.

WHICH ANCESTORS DO I WANT TO WORK WITH?

Time to discover something about working with the different types of ancestors. Remember that the group of ancestors you work with today is going to change over the course of time. You always have the choice of working with whomever you choose—or not. This spread is just an intro to what you might expect from each of the three types of your ancestors. Think of this exercise as a version of speed dating—which contestant do you want to spend more time with right now? If you already know the answer, then you can head on over to chapter 2. If you haven't worked with tarot before or you need a refresher, you can go to appendix A for Tarot 101 anytime you need it when we start discussing spreads and the meaning of cards.

Shuffle the entire deck and draw three cards, asking what you need to know about working with each type of ancestor. Who might be best for you at this time?

Card 1. Ancestors of Blood

Card 2. Ancestors of Place

Card 3. Ancestors of Time

When I was working with this spread, my card draws were The Emperor, Ace of Cups, and The Chariot.

THE EMPEROR.   ACE ↑ CUPS.   THE CHARIOT.

As you can see, it's possible that all cards are "positive." What you need to decide at this point is not only which type of ancestor it's best for you to begin working with *at this time*, but also what you're likely to encounter.

I felt like the Emperor (Blood) would help me in creating a solid foundation for my life or work; the Ace of Cups (Place) was alluring as it comes from ancestors who want to help me be more open to emotions. The Chariot (Time) is all geared up and ready to explore other lives and other times.

Now, *before making a decision*, draw three more cards, one for each type of ancestor. The question to ask is: What impact will working with this type of ancestor have on my life *at this time*?

This second draw of three may change which direction you decide to take. It did for me.

Although there were two enticing Majors in my first draw, I originally wanted to work with Ancestors of Place (Ace of Cups). However, when I looked at the impact each would have, my next three cards were: Magician (Blood), Tower (Place), and Sun (Time). Can you guess which one I chose? Which would you pick?

Journal Prompts

1. I drew _____, _____, and
_____ for the types of ancestors. For the
impact I drew _____, _____, and
_____.

2. I decided to work with _____. Here's why:

   _____

   _____

   _____

   _____ .

3. What surprised me was _____

   _____

   _____ .

Chapter 2

Working With a Spirit Guide

I f you've been doing spiritual work for any period of time, you may already have a Spirit Guide or angelic being you call on for assistance. Do you want one for Ancestral Tarot? I vote yes.

Here's the deal: Ancestral Tarot work can be done without a Spirit Guide. In fact, I worked with the ancestors for years before it occurred to me to connect. Duh.

In my experience, though, having a Spirit Guide—especially one who was family at one point in time—has been invaluable, particularly when it comes to navigating the choppy waters off Ancestor Island. I find myself calling on my guide far more often than I anticipated.

THE VOLUNTEER

When I knew I was going to write this book, it was clear I would need help from the ancestors. I sorted my tarot deck, separating out all the Court cards. I then drew a card, asking for who among the family wanted to be my guide for the duration of this book. The card I drew was the Queen of Cups, so I had a good idea it was a mature woman.

I then did a meditation, during which I asked if a guide wanted to come forward. To be honest, I expected to see my mother. But up popped a woman who told me she was my Great-grandmother Josie. I remembered seeing photos of her when I was a kid, but of course, I had never met her since she passed over long before I was born.

In retrospect, Josie was an interesting ancestor to come forward, as I remembered a story about her having a psychic connection to my dad. Hmm.

But being the skeptic, I wanted proof that Josie's appearance was for real and not something I was imagining. I asked her, in meditation, to give me a sign during the coming week. She simply said, "Look for the half-dollars." I thought, "No way." When is the last time you saw a half-dollar? Like never.

Later that same week, while dusting my bookcase, what do you think I found sitting behind a stack of books? Yep, two vintage half-dollars that I had bought years earlier. Apparently, I had stuck them behind the books and forgot all about them. Case closed. Josie became the ancestor to guide me through this book.

How to Find Your Guide

I've been doing family research for decades, so I know a lot of ancestral names. You may know absolutely nothing about your family or just the names of your parents and grandparents. If you're adopted, you may not know even that. It's all perfectly okay. Not knowing names isn't going to prevent you from making connections. Nor will it keep you from finding your guide.

There are several ways to do this, but I've focused on two that I think work well. Regardless of which method you choose, before doing anything else, first be clear on *why you want a guide* and *how you want that guide to help you*. My request was for a guide who could answer ancestral questions that came up while writing. You may want a guide for healing, protection, or magical work.

Method 1. Pick a Single Court Card

Begin by separating out all the Court cards. I almost never interpret a Court by age/gender—e.g., a young male for a Page—but in this instance I did. Go ahead and shuffle your Courts with the intent of identifying a guide, then pull a card.

If you're hazy on the Courts, use this simple chart to narrow down who is coming forward for you.

Rank	Motto	Traditional
King	I know	Mature Male
Queen	I nurture	Mature female
Knight	I quest	Adolescent
Page	I learn	Youth

If you're a visual type, look at all the Court cards pictured on page 16. You may spot someone whose energy seems compatible to yours. Trust yourself about which ancestor is drawing your attention.

Once you've identified an individual by gender and age, ask this person who wants to be your family Spirit Guide to come forward.

If you're a longtime meditator, you probably want to meditate before asking. If you don't meditate, give yourself a few minutes to close your eyes and take several deep, cleansing breaths. This isn't a race, so take your time.

Next, envision the energy running up from the Earth through your feet, then up your legs, and into your entire body. Once it reaches the top of your head, envision the energy running back down into the Earth. If you do this a few times, you will feel a calmness in your middle (solar plexus). Now, silently ask for an ancestor to step forward who wants to work with you in whichever way you've specified.

Once a volunteer makes themselves known, thank them, then ask for their name. If you don't get a name, ask for their relationship to you. You may get something like "I was a distant cousin" or "your great-great-grandpa

PAGE of WANDS.

KNIGHT of WANDS.

QUEEN of WANDS.

KING of WANDS

PAGE of SWORDS.

KNIGHT of SWORDS.

QUEEN of SWORDS.

KING of SWORDS.

PAGE of PENTACLES.

KNIGHT of PENTACLES.

QUEEN of PENTACLES.

KING of PENTACLES.

PAGE of CUPS.

KNIGHT of CUPS.

QUEEN of CUPS.

KING of CUPS.

and my great-great-grandpa were brothers." Or you could get something as vague as: "I don't know the relationship, but I'm your ancestor."

When a volunteer steps forward, ask for verification or for a sign, like I did with Josie. If you're not a skeptic, you may not need to ask for anything beyond their name or relationship.

Tip: On the whole, I don't believe ancestors lie to us with malice; I do, however, think that sometimes their sense of time and our sense of time are so different that naming an exact relationship might not mean much to them.

If you do ask for a sign, what happens if you don't get proof? Ask again. It's possible that you're getting proof, but it comes in a form different from the one you imagined. On one occasion when I was working with an ancestor, he told me to look for the red balloons. So of course, I was looking around in the sky for red balloons. But they weren't in the sky . . . they were illustrations in a children's book. I swear, I think the ancestors team up with the Faeries when it comes to pulling our legs.

Don't forget to note your guide's Court card in your journal. This is a great time to journal about how you asked for the guide, how they appeared to you, any conversation the two of you had, or any messages they brought.

Method 2. Spirit Guide Spread

For this method, you will need the Courts separated from the rest of the deck, but *only* for the first card in the spread. After drawing Card 1, place all the Courts back in the full deck and shuffle well. Now you can draw the other four cards from the entire deck. Arrange them as shown on page 18.

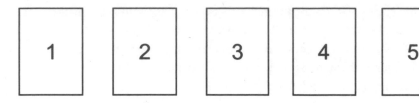

Card 1. Who is my Spirit Guide? (Draw from the Courts.)

Card 2. What message does my guide have about my Ancestral
Tarot journey?

Card 3. How can I better listen to my guide?

Card 4. Is there a side of the family that my guide wants to
help me with?

Card 5. Is there a specific family issue my guide can help with?

Why I Don't Insist on a Specific Person as a Guide

Although I can't describe exactly what the afterlife is like, I can tell you my
sense about it based on decades of working with those who have passed over.

I believe that once a soul has left this incarnation, they move on to a
different dimension where, like us, they have time to reflect on their life,
do tasks, and even go on to higher learning. I have never had a sense that
Grandma H. was around; it always felt as though she had gone on to get her
doctoral degree—or whatever the afterlife equivalent of that would be.

In my dad's case, his death was so sudden and psychically violent—
at least to me—that I see him curled up, sleeping. I have no sense when
he will reincarnate, if ever, although I do get messages from him—almost
always via the Star (Major Arcana 17).

My belief is that each soul, upon passing, has its own journey. By calling—or insisting on—a specific person to help, you could be pulling that
person off their own path. That's why I always ask that the ancestor who
wants to work with me on a specific issue come forward.

Keep in mind, as you do ancestral work, that your Spirit Guide may change. While Josie is the spirit who came forward to help with this book, I'm also aware of John, who wants to help guide me to my maternal ancestors. There are others who want to come forward too, but for me working with one at a time is a better fit for my nature. You may find a different arrangement is the best fit for you.

Guides will change, depending on your needs.

When You Don't Know What a Card Means

What if you draw a Court card and can't figure out what ancestor it might represent? Even if you know tarot well, there are times you look at a card and think, "I have absolutely no idea what ancestor this might be." This can be especially frustrating when you're doing your best to understand the sometimes subtle messages from the ancestors or even have a sense of what ancestor might be coming forward.

If this issue comes up for you, identify and analyze the card's symbols to see if things make more sense. I know that sometimes it's difficult to process all the tiny details in a card. That's why I'm a fan of tarot apps. Once I have an app, I can easily increase the size of the card until I can look at every tiny bit. See appendix B for app resources.

Using the Queen of Wands as an example, here's one way of using a card's symbols to get a better grasp on what it's all about. I've placed an arrow on almost every feature of the card that relates to Fire (Wands). They are: The lions on the back of the throne, the sunflowers on the back of the throne, the lion heads on each side of her throne, the sunflower in her left hand, and the black cat sitting at her feet. Finally, although it's a little hard to see, her cape is held together with a lion's head broach.

When you look at this card in color, you'll see that her gown as well as the distant mountains and the throne lions are all gold. Almost every symbol relates to Fire. If you know a little astrology, you'll remember that Leo (the Lion) has the Sun as its ruling planet.

What symbol in this card doesn't represent *only* Fire? The black cat. He brings in the fire of the lion but adds an additional component of intuition. What do you think happens when you throw an intuitive together with fire energy? That alone tells you a lot about this Queen.

The Queen of Wands absolutely brings a positive influence to life, her fiery energy prompting action. However, thanks to that cat, her sometimes impulsive actions can be directed based on what she is intuiting about the situation.

If the Queen of Wands comes forward, how would you interpret her? Who do you think she is? In real life, would you see her as someone who would stay home and feed you chicken soup when you're sick? Probably not. But she would be the one to push you out of your comfort zone, even if you went kicking and screaming. She nurtures your adventurous self.

If you draw this Queen, what ancestor do you think she represents?

How to Call Your Guide

Spirit Guides don't like to be ordered around any more than you do. I suggest when you need to contact a guide, you enter your inner or outer sacred space, then politely ask if your guide will come forward. If they don't, my assumption is that they're busy doing something else. They aren't my servants, and I don't believe in treating them that way.

Once you've found your first family Spirit Guide, have a conversation with them, asking if they know other family members who might want to help in your ancestral work. Also ask if there's a good time of day for your work together. I'm all for being polite.

In addition, there will be times when one of your guides tells you that they aren't appropriate for the type of work you want to do. Honor that, and ask if there's another ancestor who would like to help on that particular issue.

If you've lived long enough, you will have met people who aren't blood relatives but are family nevertheless. You know the old saying about the family you were born with and the family you acquire throughout your life? It's true. Some friends become family.

If a spirit comes forward who isn't a blood relative, but instead is someone you were incredibly close to, that's great. Ask them how they can help you with this work, then thank them for coming forward.

WORKING WITH YOUR GUIDE

As you go deeper into Ancestral Tarot work, it's likely that you'll want to invite more ancestors onto your team. I have created, while inner journeying, my own version of a Council of Elders. These are the ones in Spirit (human and nonhuman) who came forward when I asked for help.

Members of the Council are volunteers who can come and go at will. In fact, once a "job" is complete, the one who helped with it often gets up from where they've been sitting and walks off down a trail.

If you haven't created an Inner Sacred Space or taken an inner journey, now is a good time to do that. If you don't know where to begin, refer to chapter 11.

In my own meditative journey, I go to a place with many portals. One of them is a wooden door that leads into a forest. Beyond the door is a clearing and a fire ring. There I can find the ones in spirit who have come forward to work with me. Three of them are always there while others come and go.

As you continue this work, your journeys will take you to places you may not recognize or even conceptualize. Your guides may live in a cave, up a tree, in a spaceship, in an old urban building, or under the sea. If you see your stuffy and staid Uncle Mart in a tree house, climb up and join him.

I will say this one word of warning, though. I personally have never experienced an ancestor who wanted to lead me into danger or darkness. I am very well-protected by my own Spirit Guides, so this won't happen. However, if you've never worked with Spirit before, take time to set up some ground rules about what is okay and not okay. You may want to surround yourself with white light, or appoint a Spirit Guide whose sole function is to protect you. Although you're working with the ancestors, don't be surprised if an animal appears who wants to join the Protection Squad. If you've ever experienced the aggressiveness of a raccoon, you'll understand how intimidating they can be and why they might want to be part of your team. And maybe, as you continue the work, you'll wonder why you didn't call on raccoon earlier.

Depending on your background, you may want to say a prayer or mantra before beginning the work. The important thing is to set up a clear boundary so that no one of a lesser vibration can enter your presence. How you word this or the rules you choose are yours to make. All I ask is that you make them. (See the references for more on this topic.)

This is a good time to stop reading and locate your guide.

Teamwork Spread

Now that you've met your Spirit Guide, do this simple three-card spread using the entire deck. It's all about teamwork.

Ask your guide (by name): "_____, how can we best work together?" Pull three cards and interpret them as a whole.

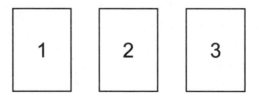

For example, my cards were The Magician, The Moon, and the Five of Cups.

I felt like I was being asked to be patient (my Aries Moon makes that difficult), to believe that together we can manifest the best book possible (Magician), and to allow Josie to guide me as I work with past losses (Five of Cups)—even if I don't understand where or why she's leading me. Most important of the three, for me, was the message that the book was going to lead me down pathways I never imagined (Moon). It has.

JOURNAL PROMPTS

1. My cards in the Teamwork Spread were:

   1. _____ 2. _____

   3. _____

2. Here's how I interpret those cards: _____

   _____ .

3. The card I found most confusing or helpful was
   _____ . I think that's because

   _____

   _____ .

Sacred Tools: Prayer

Working with ancestors is so deeply personal for me that without thinking I say a prayer before doing the work. Sometimes it's a prayer to my mother, sometimes it's to the Great Spirit, and other times it's to all my ancestors.

Prayer is a personal thing. If you were raised in a traditional religion, prayers like the 23rd Psalm or the Lord's Prayer may be familiar to you. If your upbringing was in a family of religious extremism, prayers may be the last thing you want to think about.

Depending on your particular situation, you may want to begin and end your ancestral work by addressing God, the gods, a goddess, a Higher Power, a saint, the ancestors, Great Spirit, or no one.

If you've never given much thought to prayer, in its simplest form it's a communication between you and the entity you worship. In ancestral work, you might want to use prayer to offer up thanksgiving or a request for healing.

When you think about prayer, it isn't just a Western European Christianity thing. People around the globe pray in more ways than I could ever count. Pick one that you feel a kinship to, even if you don't belong to that group. Although not a Navajo, I'm particularly fond of *Walk in Beauty* from the Blessingway Ceremony. Here's a short excerpt:

> *In beauty I walk*
> *With beauty before me I walk*
> *With beauty behind me I walk*
> *With beauty above me I walk*
> *With beauty around me I walk*
> *It has become beauty again*

This prayer reminds me to treasure all that I've been blessed with. It's also beautiful to use before ancestral work.

In Tanzania, part of a prayer asking for a cure for an illness contains these lines:

> *All ancestors, male and female, great and small,*
> *Help us in this trouble, have compassion on us;*
> *So that we can also sleep peacefully.*

As you can see, prayer takes many forms.

But what if prayer isn't your thing? If that's you, then draw three cards, asking for how best to approach ancestral work in a *sacred way*. I drew these three cards for that very question.

How would you interpret them?

Chapter 3

Tools for the Journey

You now have a Spirit Guide, and you've learned the three types of ancestors you'll be working with. So now let's dig into the tools you're going to use—and there are many.

TAROT DECKS

Throughout this book you'll see spreads illustrated with the Rider-Waite-Smith (RWS) deck. If you're new to tarot, be sure to check appendix A for Tarot 101. For now, though, what you need to know is that at its most basic, tarot is a symbolic system. Each card has symbols tucked in every which way. Look at the traditional Ten of Pentacles, for example, and you'll see that the pentacles are arranged in the same design as the Kabbalistic Tree of Life. Slick, huh?

Everything depicted on a tarot card has meaning: colors, postures, scenes, numbers, flowers, shoes, directions. Is a book just a book or is it a Book of Shadows? Why does a Page have a bunch of firecrackers hanging from her belt (Robin Wood Tarot, Page of Wands)? Why does one card show a full moon while another a waning crescent? And what's the deal with different colors of gemstones?

Learning tarot's symbolism can be a lifetime assignment. But you already knew that, didn't you?

To work through the rest of this book you're going to need at least one tarot deck, and since you'll be working with both sides of your family, you'll probably want a separate deck for each—or multiple decks.

There are exercises throughout the book that require you to separate your deck into three piles: Minor Arcana, Courts, and Major Arcana. If you have more than one deck, I suggest keeping one separated into the three piles. It's a time-saver—plus once the three piles are created you have to shuffle like crazy to make sure all the cards are reintegrated.

Although the illustrations in this book are from a standard RWS Tarot, the decks you choose for ancestral work should be the ones that you feel are most appropriate for you and your family lineage. I personally like working with a basic RWS, the Robin Wood Tarot, and the Universal Waite Tarot.

One thing's for sure: there's no lack of fascinating decks to choose from. Most retain the structure of RWS, but can vary in theme: think Faeries, unicorns, Halloween, collage, cats, and modern art. While I'm in love with many cat decks, they don't scream "ancestors!" to me—but they may for you.

In addition to varying themes, some decks change the name of certain cards or rename suits. In the Brady Tarot, for example, suits are renamed Arrows, Feathers, Horns, and Roots. In the Gaian Tarot, the Emperor becomes the Builder, while the Hierophant is the Teacher. If these work best for you, go for it.

Want more culturally based decks? Check out the Ancestral Path Tarot; its suits are illustrated with images of Arthurian England, Japan, Egypt, and Native America. Or pick a deck for ancestral work related to your own lineage. You may prefer a deck that reflects your family's origin. There are several cultural decks, like the Russian Tarot of St. Petersburg, Celtic Tarot, Santa Muerte Tarot, Tarot Illuminati, and Dust II Onyx: A Melanated Tarot. If English is not your first language, you may like decks, such as those published by Lo Scarabeo, that are titled in English, Spanish, French, Italian, and German.

More regionally specific (and sometimes obscure) decks can be found by Googling tarot + the country of origin. These include but are not limited to:

- African American Tarot (African American)
- African Tarot (Africa)
- Afro Tarot (Africa)
- Arthurian Tarot (Britain)
- Aum Tarot (Hindu/Ayurvedic)
- China Tarot (China)
- Chinese Tarot (China)
- Druidcraft Tarot (Celtic)
- Ghetto Tarot (Haiti)
- Hazel Moon's Hawaiian (Hawaii/Polynesia)
- Hoodoo Tarot (African America)
- Javanese Folktales Tarot (Java/Indonesia)
- Legitimo Tarot (Brazil)
- Llewellyn Tarot (Wales)
- Medicine Woman Tarot (Modern Native American—Female Centric)
- Modern Witch (Wicca)
- Native American Tarot (Native American)
- New Orleans Voodoo Tarot (African Diaspora)
- Polski Tarot (Poland)
- Raymond Buckland's Romani Tarot (Romani/Romanichal)
- Raziel (Jewish)
- Santa Fe Tarot (Navajo)
- Spanish Tarot (Spain)

- Tarot Français Des Fleurs (France)

- Tarot of the Moors (Andalusia/Spain)

- Tarot of the Old Path (Pagan)

- Tarot of the Orishas (Africa and African Diaspora)

- Tarot Piatnik (French Marseilles)

- Ukiyoe Tarot (Japan)

- Vikings Tarot (Norse)

Whichever decks you use—and I do encourage you to experiment—be aware that the theme and style of the deck are going to lend an energy to both your interpretation of the cards and the ancestral messages.

That said, if you're the type of tarot reader who goes strictly by the book, then regardless of deck, you're going to read a traditional Three of Wands exactly the same way you'd read a nontraditional Three of Wands.

While I know tarot-by-the-book, I use the basics as a foundation, but then jump off based on the card's energy. I let the image and the colors merge with my own energy, and most importantly, I just listen to what they say. But that's just how I read. Because of that, my choice of deck is critically important.

The bottom line is how we read the cards is going to impact the messages. There is no right or wrong, just what works for you.

And, lest I forget, here's a word about reversals—cards that fall upside down. Personally, I don't read reversals—*unless I do*. I know that sounds like a cop-out, but I read more intuitively than bookishly, which means I don't read them with an upside down interpretation, unless I feel that I should. Then I do. Confusing, I know. If you are a traditionalist, by all means, look at reversals as blocked or imbalanced energy for that card, but in working with the ancestors don't feel tied to that if another message is coming through. Go with your own system of reading reversals, whatever that might be.

Tarot Spreads

Each chapter has at least one tarot spread. That doesn't mean you can't create your own. As you work your way through this family journey, your questions for the ancestors are going to be far different from mine or anyone else's.

In this section I'm going to show you how to create or modify a spread to fit your own needs.

Spread Basics

As you do the exercises or read through each section, several questions will pop up. Some are questions you'll be asking yourself; others are questions you want to send out to the ancestors. When the questions come up, write them down in your journal. As you finish each chapter, use your own questions to create a personally relevant spread or modify the one that I've suggested.

Another thing you'll want to consider is how to strategically lay out the cards—in what order and in what design. Here's a sample of what I'm talking about: I wanted to know why an ancestor passed over not long after his birth.

My questions were

1. Why did you die?

2. Why were you born?

3. What lesson is your brief life and death for me?

4 What did your life and death mean for the family?

5. Do you have a message for me?

In creating this spread, I could simply lay five cards down in a horizontal row, but I didn't. Here's why. The design of a tarot spread *has its own energy*. And here I wanted the energy to reflect my confusion over why this ancestor had passed over so early.

This was the spread design I created. I also could also have shuffled, peeled off five cards, then tossed them in the air and let Spirit decide which card went with which of the five questions.

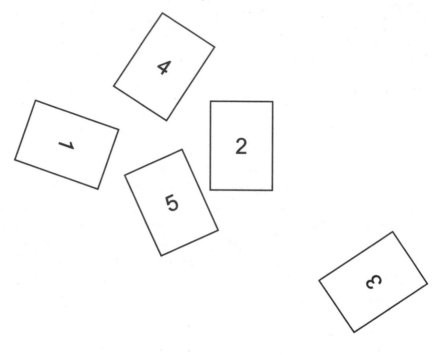

Types of Spread Designs

The most common spread designs are vertical or horizontal lines, crossing lines, grids, bridges, circles, or two paths (used for exploring two options). Some spreads, like the Celtic Cross, are built using horizontal lines, vertical lines, and a crossing line.

For me, a card design is a blueprint for telling a story. A linear spread becomes a chronological narrative. A circular spread is a narrative that takes me back to the beginning, but with more knowledge than when I began. In a three-card spread with the middle card turned horizontally, the middle card is a bridge between the left and right cards. In a spread such as a classic Celtic Cross, we're seeing "crossing cards" as obstacles, far left as the past, the tenth card as the future—we are simply following a narrative from the beginning to its conclusion. Add to this the flow of energy. If you want to understand a disjointed story (like mine earlier), your spread is probably not going to be linear. Trust your instincts.

As you work with the ancestors, I know you are going to discover the exact right spread design to match the energy of your questions.

If you're wondering why most of the spreads in this book are created using a simple horizontal line, it's just a way of saving space.

A quick word about tarot definitions and interpretations. Although there are who-knows-how-many tarot books, each with the author's absolute definition of each card, I'm not that keen on being so regimented.

It's fine to look up card meanings, but be open to using your intuition. For example, look at the traditional Ten of Wands. At a quick glance, is he struggling under the load, or is he hurrying along, anxious to get the wands home to begin building his new house?

See the nice house in the background? Do you think it's his or is he a workman on someone's estate? We know that the man is weighed down, but we don't know why or whether he's okay with it. Maybe he wants to dump the Wands and walk away. This is where your intuition comes in, along with other cards in a spread. Don't be afraid to toss what the book says and listen to the message you're receiving.

Ancestral Tarot work is often not "by the book." Give yourself permission to jump off the Fool's cliff and trust that your jump was Divine.

Fairy Tales & Baseball Players?

Regardless of which deck you choose for this work, you may get tripped up by either some of the Courts or the Majors. For me, the Minor Arcana cards are probably the easiest to interpret as they're an open window into an ancestor's everyday life.

If you're having problems relating a Court or Major to one of your ancestors, I suggest creating your own cards to take the place of the tarot cards that are giving you fits. If you want to replace all seventy-eight cards with your own versions, I'm impressed.

As an example of how to riff off the norm, one of the charms of the Inner Child Tarot deck, published about thirty years ago, was that the Majors were recognizable fairy-tale characters. The Chariot became Peter Pan while the High Priestess was pictured as the Fairy Godmother. If you love fairy tales, why not create cards based on fairy tales to replace the hard-to-interpret ones?

If your family wasn't the fairy-tale type (unless you're talking about the Wicked Stepmother), how about using images from baseball, urban settings, collages, plants, or whatever matches your family? You can even give cards new names if you like—*as long as the cards carry the same intent as the traditional deck and as long as you can relate them to your ancestors.*

Card-Making Made Easy

If you want to replace a handful of traditional cards, here's the down and dirty way to get all DIY-y.

1. Gather a set of blank cards (you can buy them on *Amazon.com* or at gaming card companies) or you can use blank index cards.

2. Decide on a theme or alternative names.

3. If you're an artist, you are so lucky. Design away.

4. If the artist gene skipped over your DNA, pull out those old magazines and find the appropriate imagery, then start gluing them to the blank cards.

Oh yeah, I almost forgot. If you're already into crafty scrapbook stuff, I bet you have one of those punch-out thingies that round corners. If so, round off the corners of index cards and they'll look like a real card.

I joke that my mother never read me fairy tales—something she always denied—so I decided to remake three cards I'm not fond of: the Wheel of Fortune, Temperance, and the Devil, but not in fairy-tale format.

As I've always seen the Devil as the one who lures us into addictive patterns, I made a card picturing a pile of doughnuts—my personal downfall. I understand, of course, that doughnuts themselves are not the Devil, but the road they can lead me down is diabolical.

As for Temperance, I found a picture of a bunch of laboratory vials. That's because I see Temperance as an alchemist—looking for the exact right blend of ingredients (experiences) that will turn lead into gold. Temperance is not just pouring things from one cup to another willy-nilly; there's a method to the madness.

And, of course, my Wheel became a Native American Medicine Wheel. For me the Medicine Wheel with its symbolic colors and associated animals better represents the cycles we experience as we go through life than the ever-turning Wheel of Fortune.

At another time, because I am a baseball fan, I created an oracle deck with a baseball theme. My Hanged Man was a photograph of stop-motion: a player sliding into a base, the baseman waiting for the throw, and the umpire yet to make the call. A perfect suspended moment.

Making or renaming tarot cards isn't just about having an afternoon of crafty fun. As you work to create your own cards, the energy of your creation will begin to mesh with your own. When complete, you'll find that you intuitively understand the card better than ever before. Using your own cards in an ancestral reading is just one more way to add a layer of information to the work.

Don't put those scissors away yet. Later in the book I'll be showing you how to make meaningful ancestral cards.

TAROT & SIGILS

Tarot's not the only symbolic system we're going to work with. Next up is sigil-making. If you haven't worked with a sigil before, you're in for a treat. A sigil, just like a tarot card, is a symbolic representation of a person, place, intent, idea, or desire. Just as a tarot card can be used ritualistically, so can a sigil.

At its most basic, a sigil is a design created to express a desire. It can be simple—such as a heart shape—or complex—combining multiple shapes, letters, or even numbers. Sigils are often designed to attract love, money, or work or to achieve a specific goal.

Before we get into three sigil-making techniques, let's gather some source material for creating an ancestral sigil.

First, pull a tarot card from the whole deck, asking for the card that best blends with your ancestral work. Using that card as inspiration, you're going to generate a sigil.

Note: You can also draw from only the Majors, if you prefer. It's entirely up to you.

It's easy to create a sigil design based on a "positive" card like the Star or the Nine of Cups. But what if you draw what you consider a "negative" card like the Five of Pentacles or the Five of Cups? Simple. Use the imagery from

the card to inspire your sigil design. For example, the Five of Cups is near the water, which is symbolic of healing, so use water in some way as part of your design. Remember the wavy water lines you drew to represent water when you were a kid? That works.

The Five of Pentacles shows a church window, which is all about the sacred. That means sacredness would be the focus for your sigil. Or it might also inspire you to create your sigil in a place that is sacred to you.

When you draw a tarot card for sigil work, ask the ancestors for the card that best complements the Ancestral Tarot work you want to do.

Sigil Techniques

There are several methods and schools of thought around sigil design and use—just search YouTube or Google for "how to make a sigil" and you can watch sigil-making ad infinitum.

For the purposes of Ancestral Tarot, though, I'm going to show you three sound techniques to use with the card you pulled, then we'll talk about how to create the sigil and how to activate it.

Sigil Method 1. Free-Form Letters

Probably one of the most popular methods of creating a sigil design is to write your intent on a piece of paper, keeping it to one sentence. It's important that you be ultra-focused and crystal clear about your desire. In this case, you'll be making a sigil for ancestral work based on the tarot card you just pulled.

If your card was one that you associate with healing (like the water in the Five of Cups), your intent may be something like *I am healing through ancestral work*. Once you're satisfied with your statement of intent, write it on a piece of paper. Again, short and sweet works best.

Next, cross out all the vowels and double letters. I've eliminated I-a-e-a-i-o-u-a-e-a-o. Because there are double letters, I've also eliminated the repeats h-n-l-t-r.

That leaves m h l n g t r c s w k.

Now comes the fun: using the remaining letters, draw them inside a circle in any way you like. You can be as creative as you want. That means you can draw letters backward or turn an *n* into an *m*, make a *t* out of an *l*. If you like, you can also add a curving line to represent the water.

Because I'm always drawn to a simple approach, instead of using the sentence "I am healing through ancestral work," I choose to work only with the word *healing*. Using this first technique, I removed the vowels, leaving me with the letters: h-l-n-g. This is what I created.

Once you're satisfied with your design, you can leave your sigil drawn on a piece of paper or you can draw it on other surfaces like a stone or glass.

Some people like to draw the sigil on their body, get a sigil tattoo, or carve it into a candle or the soap with which they bathe. I woodburned mine onto a small wooden disc for no other reason than that I prefer wood to other media.

If you don't have access to wood for cutting out discs, most craft stores carry packets of them. Interestingly, the last time I saw them in a craft store they were cut from birch. Do you think the craft company realized that birch is a magical tree, known to represent new beginnings as well as ward off evil? I kinda doubt it.

Sigil Method 2. The Number Square

This is my preferred method, as I spent a lot of years doing numerology. In this method you first assign letters to the numbers 1-9:

1	2	3	4	5	6	7	8	9
a, j, s	b, k, t	c, l, u	d, m, v	e, n, w	f, o, x	g, p, y	h, q, z	i, r

Now, instead of writing a whole sentence, choose one word—or two at most—that symbolizes your intent. In this example, my word was *healing*. Using the number-letter table above, *healing* converts to 8513957.

To create this sigil, just draw in the square from number to number, starting with the first letter and ending with the last. It's common to place a

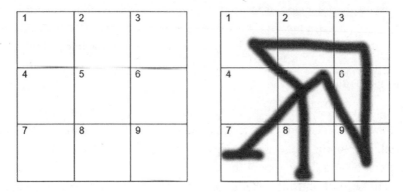

circle at the beginning number and a short straight line at the end. You can eliminate doubles like the fives if you choose, but I decided to keep them.

Again, my word was *healing* = 8513957.

As you can see, I started in the 8 square with a small circle and ended in the 7 with a horizontal line. Once you've created a sigil within the square, copy the design onto your media of choice.

Sigil Method 3. Simple Symbols

This is an easy method. Shuffle your tarot deck with the intent of drawing a card whose energies match that of your ancestral work energies. Once you've drawn a card, pull an image or part of an image from the card that speaks to you. Then, create your sigil by drawing that imagery. This way your sigil will be energetically connected to your tarot card.

For the Five of Cups, this might mean creating a circle within which you draw waves or cups. For the Five of Pentacles, what is sacred to you? I might choose to symbolically represent trees in a forest because, for me, the forest is sacred. You may use a pentacle or the shape of the stained-glass windows.

If the Two of Cups (the card of deep friendship or love), you might incorporate symbols to represent feelings, eternity, or growth. Perhaps something like this with a heart for feelings, the infinity symbol for eternity, and a stylized tree for growth:

If you are drawn to this technique, why not sketch symbols in your journal and key words for each. This makes them uniquely yours. Go ahead and create the sigil energy that matches you and your Ancestral Tarot intent.

Charging Your Sigil

Charging a sigil is like adding a battery to the Energizer Bunny (thank you, Andrew Kyle McGregor). There are two schools of thought about charging a sigil. The first is that the very act of creating the sigil is charging it with your energy and the energy of the Universe.

The second and more commonly held belief is that a ritual is done following the creation and the ritual is the charging element. I actually fall into the first school of thought.

If you prefer creating ritual, a common one is drawing your sigil on a piece of paper, entering a meditative or quiet, undistracted state, then lighting a candle. After energetically placing your emotional and psychic energy into the sigil, burn the paper. This sends the energy out into the Universe.

There is no right-or-wrong way to charge a sigil—it's really all about your intent. Other methods include:

- If you live by water, draw the sigil in sand or earth and let the water carry it away.

- Eat food that has your sigil carved into it.

- Draw your sigil using powder, then blow it away. (It's best to do this one outdoors.)

- Bury the sigil, with an intent that the Earth Mother will take your intent to heart.

- Fill the sigil with your emotional, mental, and spiritual intent, then place it somewhere sacred to you.

- Some people charge their sigils during sex—think of the tremendous energy flowing out into the sigil.

You can also activate your sigil with an act from your heart. Before I began writing this book, I woodburned a sigil that was a combination of my parents' initials. I then left the sigil on their tombstone after saying a prayer and petitioning them for help. Standing there, I could feel the immense emotional power of what I had created. The energy was so overwhelming it made my entire body tingle.

If you're ready to create your sigil, you can stop reading here and draw your tarot card, then set your intent (be as clear as possible), and generate your sigil using one of the three methods. Or if you want to incorporate moon energy, read on.

Sigils and the Moon

One additional thing you may want to incorporate into your sigil work is the phase of the moon.

I like creating a sigil corresponding with the moon phase of my natal chart, a waning gibbous. If you're connected to moon energy or work your magic by moon phases like Granny did when planting vegetables, this might be something you want to incorporate as well.

If you don't know the phase of the moon under which you were born, Google "which phase of the moon was I born under?" Both MoonGiant.com and Astrocal.co.uk have simple calculators, while Astrostyle.com takes into account your time and place of birth, giving you not only the phase of the moon but also your astrological Moon sign. This information will come in handy when working with birth dates of ancestors as well. More on that later.

An equally auspicious time to activate your sigil is when the astrological sign the moon is passing through is the same as your own Moon sign. Extra points if it's a full or new moon, e.g., the full moon in Cancer for someone with a natal Cancer moon. Double extra points if you are activating your sigil during a lunar eclipse taking place in your Moon sign. While eclipse energy is powerful, you may not want to wait for one—there are only two (sometimes three) lunar eclipses per year. I won't experience a lunar eclipse in my own Moon sign until 2033!

In the course of this work, I've made some amazing progress establishing a deeper connection with the ancestors during certain phases of the moon or during a phase that was important in the life of an ancestor.

For example, if you know the birth date of an ancestor, use the moon phase calculator to discover which phase of the moon they were born under or their Moon sign.

Both my mom and dad were born under a waning gibbous moon, as I was. To me, that's a perfect time for Ancestral Tarot work, for building a tarot-based crystal grid (see chapter 11), or other magical practices.

Lunar Energies

Every twenty-eight days or so, the moon goes from dark to full and back again.

- The moon phase between dark and full is called a waxing moon.

- From the full moon to the dark moon is a waning moon.

- If the moon is less than half lit, it's called a crescent moon.

- If more than half lit, it's known as a gibbous moon.

If you see the phrase *waxing gibbous*, you know that the moon is about three-quarters lit on its way from dark to full. NASA made a nifty chart as a reference: *solarsystem.nasa.gov.*

What Do the Phases Mean?

New Moon. Plant the seeds for whatever new thing you want. This is an auspicious day to write out your ancestral "want" list. In this case, I'd use it as a time to clearly state your desires around ancestral work—whether it's honoring them, building an altar, or doing healing. This is also a time during which I'd call in an ancestor for help in initiating a project. Also draw a tarot card as a focus for your ancestral work.

Waxing Moon. At this time, the moon is building to full, so it's a perfect phase to pour your energy into your new moon intent. You might also consider charging your sigil during a waxing moon.

Full Moon. Hopefully this is a time when your intent comes to fruition. If it has not, draw another card asking for clarification.

Waning Moon. During this time of winding down and release, thank the ancestors for how they have helped you, then do a ritual blessing and letting go.

Another way of using tarot with moon energy is to draw one to three tarot cards and let them guide you in creating your intent. Then, from new moon through full moon and back to new again, use the entire moon cycle to work with one ancestor on one project, problem, or family pattern. Utilizing a single intent during an entire moon cycle can be profoundly powerful.

If you're not sure of a current moon phase, either Google it or use a moon app (appendix B). There are additional moon phases, but the ones I've listed are the ones most commonly referred to.

JOURNAL—PHYSICAL OR DIGITAL

I probably don't have to even say this, but if you're not journaling about your Ancestral Tarot practice, please start. For me, it's impossible to do this work without keeping a record. I admit I'm not always the best at daily journaling, but if nothing else I do write about the tarot spreads I'm working with and messages from the ancestors.

When you journal, be sure to add the date of your entry, including the year. Trust me, at some point in the future you're going to want to know the exact date that a piece of information or a connection came through. I could kick myself when I look back at journal entries and realize I didn't add the year.

Although I'm notorious for keeping notes wherever—journals, steno pads, sticky notes, and tiny booklets—I actually do keep a special journal for ancestral work. This journal includes photos of ancestors if I have them, photos or sketches of spreads that I do, cards I've drawn that seem significant, notes, insights, and messages I receive.

If, unlike me, you're lucky enough to be an artist, this is a great place for your sketches. You may even want to add drawings or photos of family in a digital journal, including distant ancestors as you imagine them, especially as photography didn't exist until the mid-nineteenth century.

A journal is also a place I use to store ideas for honoring and working with specific ancestors. For example, maybe I want to remember to leave real or virtual flowers for someone, or I may want to remember to name an ancestor in a blessing or petition. In chapter 11 I'll show you how to add virtual flowers to an ancestral tombstone even if you live thousands of miles away from the cemetery.

To be honest, for years I went back and forth between a paper and a digital journal, never quite finding the right fit. But now I use a paper journal because I finally found a brand I'm in love with. Writing in it is joyful. How about that. It really doesn't matter what kind of journal you choose. As they say—the best system is the one you'll use. So get in the journaling habit early—and in chapter 8 we'll look at more ways to incorporate your journal in your Ancestral Tarot practice.

Tarot & Pendulums

Using a pendulum with your tarot cards is totally optional, but it's something I've done for a long time and I love the added energy the pendulum brings.

Before you ask me what type of pendulum I would suggest for ancestral work, I'll pass along the answer I received when asking the same question of a local crystal expert: "It's not about which type of stone or metal the pendulum is made of, it's about picking the pendulum up and asking it if it wants to work with you and the ancestors. Trust me, the pendulum's answer will be quick and definite. I have one pendulum that's at its best when doing ancestral work. Another, not so much."

Here are a few ways I use a pendulum in Ancestral Tarot work.

After shuffling the deck, I spread the cards out in a fan, then use my ancestor pendulum to choose the cards for whatever spread I'm working on. If you've ever used a pendulum, you'll know that they can move in almost any direction: clockwise and counterclockwise, lines that go in the four cardinal directions, as well as degrees between, e.g., NNE to SSW.

Pendulums react differently for each person, and different pendulums behave differently, regardless of who is using them. One of mine tugs at my hand, while another shimmies. The more you use a pendulum, the more accurate the results. That's because with frequent use you'll be able to tell, by feel, what the pendulum is telling you. Like tarot, getting good with a pendulum requires that you practice with one.

If you have a pendulum, go ahead and fan out your deck, then use your pendulum to pick a card or cards from one of the earlier spreads. How did that feel?

A second way to use a pendulum is to find a specific card in the deck. I know, crazy. But it's good practice.

Split your deck into four more or less equal piles, then ask the pendulum which pile a specific card is in. I have one pendulum that never finds the card and another that finds it about 90 percent of the time.

Here's another cool way to use a pendulum. Split the deck into four piles then use the pendulum to pick the pile with the most energy. How will you know what "the most energy" is? Typically, the pendulum will move in a way far different over one pile than the other three. Again, work with your pendulum and let it help you learn its magical ways.

After the pile is chosen, flip over the top card, the bottom card, and the card in roughly the middle of the pile. This method works well to get an answer about an ancestral question.

Here's an example. My question was: "How can I be more consistent in doing my Ancestral Tarot work?" After the pendulum picked a pile, the top, bottom, and middle cards were:

I immediately heard: Love, Give, Honor. From those three words I wrote a personal devotion. But because I'm so practical, I wanted more information. Without drawing a clarifying card, what message might these three cards hold?

I think they are encouraging me to work more with a female ancestor in my daily practice as well as the person whom she was married to or partnered with in real life. This will be interesting as I've never worked with two ancestors at the same time.

Give this method a try, then tuck it into your journal.

Tarot & Runes

If your lineage is Northern European or if you relate to Nordic culture or even if you just love runes, you may want to turn to runes as a clarifier for a tarot draw. While many books have been written about runes (see appendix B), for our purposes they are a divination system with alphabetic symbols based on a runic alphabet. Although their exact origin is unknown, runic inscriptions have been found on objects as diverse as stones, spearheads, and jewelry, dating back at least to the third century CE. Today, runes are most typically crafted by inscribing the runic symbols on wood, glass, or stone.

- *Clarifying cards do exactly what you think they do—placed beside a confusing tarot card, they bring an extra layer of interpretation. Runes and Oracle decks are often used as clarifiers as well.*

A friend and I were working with one of the spreads from the book, and because he knew runes better than tarot, he pulled one rune to complement each tarot card. It's amazing how much deeper the interpretation is with just adding that one extra layer.

Oracle Decks

Many tarot readers use Oracle cards to clarify a tarot draw, just as they would a rune. Some Oracles blend beautifully with certain tarot decks; others feel grating. For example, I don't like using a fairy-type oracle with a black-and-white tarot deck. That might not bother you, but it jars me.

I like blending an Oracle with a tarot deck in ancestral work, just because it can add a deeper layer of understanding, just like using the runes. When it comes to working with an ancestor who lived eight or ten generations before me, I want all the information I can get.

The choice of Oracle decks is absolutely yours, but I'd encourage you to consider why you're doing this work. If your main goal in ancestral work is healing—either yourself or some of your ancestral patterns—why not look for an Oracle deck that's themed around healing. This might be some type of Angel deck—if that's your thing—or a type of lightworker's deck, an herbal oracle, or a shamanic deck. If you want to explore your ancestral origins as they relate to an ancient place, your Oracle choices might run toward earth wisdom or animals.

JOURNAL PROMPTS

1. The tarot decks I'm going to use are _____.

2. The other divinatory tools I'm going to use are

_____

_____ .

3. When I was born, my moon was in the sign of _____ and in a _____ phase.

Chapter 4

Meet the Family

However well you think you know your family members—living or not—the truth is you get only a glimpse of who they really are. We all wear masks and reveal our true selves to only a very few people during our lifetime. Using tarot as a tool to understand your current family will help you interpret the cards that you draw for your ancestors.

WHO ARE THEY, REALLY?

Although you're going to work with lots of ancestors during this book, it all starts with a simple exercise called Meet the Family. This exercise will help ground you in the practice of pulling and reading cards, journaling, and associating ancestors with specific tarot cards, elements, keywords, and a bit of astrology.

Although this may sound overwhelming, it's not.

Unless you're adopted, you probably know your parents' names as well as the names of your grandparents. You may or may not know the names of your great-grandparents. That's not a problem, as we'll also be working with ancestors you never knew or even heard of—or who lived so long ago no one remembers they even existed.

One thing I want you to know—and this is important—is that even if you have or have had difficulties with your family (we'll get into healing family patterns a little later), there are ancestors who embrace you whole-heartedly. They want to love you, protect you, help when they can, and guide you if asked.

There are also ancestors who really don't want to be involved with ancestral work. I've run into more than one ancestor who basically tells me, "no, thanks, not interested." For me, that's fine because there are plenty of others who feel exactly the opposite.

In this chapter you're going to be learning about your most immediate family, with the goal of using tarot to get a sense of personality, daily life, and major life themes.

READING A FAMILY CHART

If you've never read a family chart, they can really look confusing. In this chapter you'll be looking at two different types of charts. On the first type, marriages are denoted by a horizontal line while their children are noted with a vertical line running down from the parents' horizontal line. It looks like this.

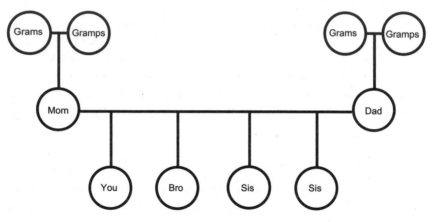

Since it's unusual these days for families to have a lot of children, the vertical lines are easy to follow. However, go back just a few generations and it becomes common to see families with ten or more children, so these charts can get kind of messy. There are reasons for this, among them:

1.   More kids equals more help on the farm.

2. High infant mortality was once common. Many children used to pass away during childhood, partly because of the lack of medical care and hygiene and partly because there was once no cure for childhood diseases such as measles, which killed thousands annually.

3. Unfortunately, due to lack of birth control, women had few options other than to birth child after child.

Not to be confusing, but I also want to introduce you to another type of chart, called a pedigree chart. This is the kind of chart most typically used in genealogy. The pedigree chart has the same information as the first chart, except it's designed more horizontally than vertically. Suffice it to say that if you want to go back several generations, it will take lots of paper. As you can see, the first chart lists you and your siblings, the second kind lists only one child—you.

How to Fill Out the Chart

To begin this exercise, pull out your journal and hand-draw a chart that looks like either of the two samples. Write in your name and the name of your parents and grandparents.

You now have a basic chart from which to work.

At this point the only thing you need to write on the chart is a name. It's okay if you want to note their relationship to you if that helps you keep them straight. Don't worry about places or dates. If your parents and/or grandparents are still living, fill in the chart anyway; this is just an exercise in pulling cards and associating them with people, living or not.

If you don't know someone's name (such as a grandparent who was out of the picture), just leave the line blank but write in the relationship, e.g., paternal (dad's side of the family) grandmother. In some cases, such as illegitimacy, you may not have a clue about the identity of a father or grandfather. In those cases, just write in the relationship to you without using a name.

Also, while you may have had a great relationship with one parent and a crummy one with the other, don't get hung up on it for this exercise. Regardless of what you thought of someone, you're going to be learning about them at a different level using your tarot cards.

As you fill in the blanks, did you happen to notice that with every generation the number of your direct ancestors doubles? (Direct ancestors are all the moms and dads but not your aunts, uncles, in-laws, siblings, or cousins).

The chart back to your grandparents shows you have two parents and (doubling) four grandparents. If we had gone back one further generation, you'd have eight great-grandparents. If another generation, then you get to sixteen. The number of your direct ancestors doubles with each preceding generation.

If you continue to double the number of your direct ancestors for twenty generations, you'll have gone back in time about five hundred years and will have over one million direct ancestors. Mind-boggling, huh? As a point of reference, that takes you to the time period of Elizabeth I, queen of England. It's unlikely you'll want to work with all of those ancestors, but if you're one of the lucky people who already knows your lineage for multiple generations, go ahead and create a chart that goes back as early in time as you choose.

Method 1. Draw a Court Card

Next, you're going to start pulling cards for each person on your chart. Start by separating your tarot deck into three piles: Minors, Courts, and Majors. You'll start with the Courts, then later in the chapter you'll pull a Minor and a Major. If the person on your chart is still alive, that's okay. Remember, this is just a warm-up.

Courts will show you personality. Minors depict everyday life. And Majors represent archetypal energy. Using all three components, you'll end up with a basic foundational sense about who the person really is or was.

Because there are a finite number of tarot cards and an infinite number of ancestors, I suggest pulling a Court for one person on your chart, writing the name of the Court on your chart, then putting the card back into the pile and reshuffling. I do this because who knows how many Knights of Cups or Queens of Swords are up your family tree? Working with all sixteen Courts gives your ancestors a chance to be tagged with the "right" card.

If you were adopted, you can use your adoptive parents as your parents, or you can draw cards for your birth parents—whichever feels right for you. It might be particularly helpful for you to investigate the personality, archetypes, and situation of your birth parents if this is something you want to know or understand.

I did a chart for my family as an example, shown on page 54. You might notice that I added one more generation, only because I happen to know who they were. But even if you don't have a clue who the ancestors are, add as many generations to your chart as you want. Just keep track of their relationship to you and which side of the family they're on.

At a Glance

Using just this Court card draw, what is there to learn? As I looked over my own chart, the first thing I noted was that Mom's side of the family were all Kings and Queens, with one Wand, four Pentacles, and two Swords. Note something missing? Yep, no Cups. Right now, before drawing any more cards, Mom's side looks like they concentrated on the practical side of life,

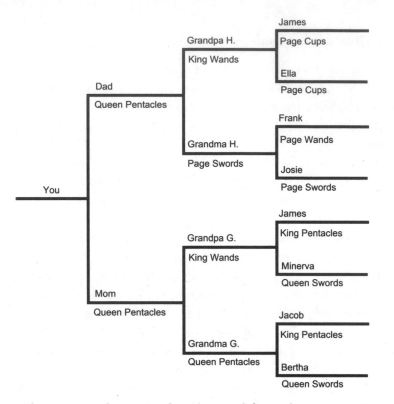

James
Page Cups

Grandpa H.
King Wands

Ella
Page Cups

Dad
Queen Pentacles

Frank
Page Wands

Grandma H.
Page Swords

Josie
Page Swords

You

James
King Pentacles

Grandpa G.
King Wands

Minerva
Queen Swords

Mom
Queen Pentacles

Jacob
King Pentacles

Grandma G.
Queen Pentacles

Bertha
Queen Swords

with pretty much zero in the warm and fuzzy department. From stories that Mom told me, that's right on.

I don't think we're looking at a family who was all that emotional or even outwardly affectionate. The focus here was on everyday things like work or home (lots of Pentacles). Does that mean Mom was a hardnose? Nope. You'll learn more about her as we draw more cards.

Now Dad's side was superinteresting. 1 King, 1 Queen, and 5 Pages. Elementally, 2 Wands, 1 Pentacle, 2 Swords, and 2 Cups.

Just by pulling Courts it looks like Mom's side of the family was really into practical things while Dad's was far more elementally balanced. Plus, with five Pages out of seven cards, Dad's side were people who were totally into learning new stuff. No wonder all of us kids turned out to be readers and lifelong learners.

Method 2. Court Cards Based on the Current Year

Thanks to the Court card expertise of Alison Cross (*Tarot-Thrones.com*), there's a second method of determining a Court card for the ancestors on your chart. By the way, this method was originally devised to discover *your* Court card for the year, but it works just fine for assigning Courts to the family.

Using this method you're going to find the Court card for an ancestor on your chart based on the *month and day of their birth* added to the current year. Reduce the total until it is 17 or less.

Here's an example: I'll start with an ancestor I know was born on August 18, and let's say I want to work with him in the year 2022. Adding 8 (August) + 18 + 2022 = 2048, which reduces to 14 (2 + 0 + 4 + 8). Using the chart below, this ancestor is wearing the cloak of the King of Cups. If I wanted to work with him in 2023 (8 + 18 + 2023 = 2049), he would take on the guise of the King of Swords (2 + 0 + 4 + 9 = 15).

If you want to follow this method even further, associate the number of the Court with the number of a Major Arcana. That would mean the energy of working with this ancestor in 2023 would be 15 (the Devil). Got it?

Page of Pentacles	17	Queen of Pentacles	9
Page of Cups	2	Queen of Cups	10
Page of Swords	3	Queen of Swords	11
Page of Wands	4	Queen of Wands	12
Knight of Pentacles	5	King of Pentacles	13
Knight of Cups	6	King of Cups	14
Knight of Swords	7	King of Swords	15
King of Wands	8	King of Wands	16

Your First Impressions

Now that you've drawn a Court for everyone on your chart (or used Alison's method), stop a sec and look for any patterns. Looking solely at the Courts, what do you find? (If you can't remember keywords or elements, use the following charts.)

What if your family tree showed six fires (Wands) or all Knights? Amazing what just a few cards can show, huh? And we haven't even gotten to the Minors and Majors. If your chart, like one of my client's, shows the women to be Kings and the men to be Pages, you may be looking at a pattern of insecure men who are more comfortable letting the women in their family lead the way.

Take a few minutes to note in your journal any first impressions. You don't need to dig deep—this is an "at a glance" impression.

Court Card Correspondences

Rank	Kings	Queens	Knights	Pages
Keywords	Clarity of mind, strategic, masters of their suit	Receptive, truthful, quietly confident	Impatient, easily bored, on a quest	Curious, quick learners, eager to experience

Using the Elemental Correspondences (below), do you find an equal number of each element throughout, or are you seeing a preponderance of one or more elements?

Elemental Correspondences

Suit	Wands	Cups	Swords	Pentacles
Element	Fire	Water	Air	Earth

What elements do you think might appear if you went back even more generations? If you want to take the time, why not draw your chart back even further and see what Courts and elements pop up? If you're willing to go back five or six generations, without even knowing any names, you'll really start to see patterns forming along family lines.

Major Arcana

Have you gathered as much info from the family Courts as possible? If so, repeat the process using only the Major Arcana (0-21). As before, after drawing a card for one person, place it back in the pile so everyone gets a chance at all the cards. These cards will show you the archetypal energies of the person's life.

Time-out to draw cards and make notes on your chart.

The cards drawn for my chart didn't show many of the lighter energies. Instead I had a bunch of Hierophants, Justices, and Judgements. For me, the Majors helped me understand why my nature is far more serious than a lot of my friends.

As you're working with two cards now, find the story that ties each to the other. If your dad was the Knight of Cups but the theme of his life was the Emperor, how did that play out in real life? What tale do the two cards tell?

Family Patterns

So far you've gotten a look at personality and major life themes. Are you surprised to see patterns already emerging? Probably not, as we're all raised by someone. How *they* were raised, for good or bad, has a direct impact on your life. And for some, that impact remains.

Here's what I mean by that: My grandmother was raised by a father who was a strict disciplinarian. Grandma's grandfather (we're going way back now) served in the Civil War (1861–1865) and was raised within the social and cultural norms of the 1800s. What does that mean for Ancestral Tarot studies? It means that the family system of how to raise kids bounced back and forth from one end of a hundred-year spectrum to the other.

Grandma could walk the straight and narrow or let loose a little. Mom could have done the same. Whose traditions were followed from one generation to the next? Grandma rebelled against the strict authority, while

Mom found a middle ground. My guess is, generationally, your family did something of the same.

It's easy to forget how very close we are to our own histories. It doesn't take many generations to get back one hundred years. Just as DNA is passed along from generation to generation, so are the customs and norms of how children "should" be raised or what family dynamics are at work. Who sticks with the program or who kicks over the traces isn't written in stone.

Those generational patterns don't have to be blatant. In fact, they can manifest in inconsequential ways. If you had walked into my mother's house and didn't remove your cap, you'd hear about it. If you objected to "the Man" always carving the Thanksgiving turkey (as I did), you'd have been given more than a side-eye.

I don't want you to think that all those family patterns are negative, though. One of my close friends is a healer, as was her grandmother and is her granddaughter. Another friend comes from a long line of public servants. He continues the work of striving for the public good. Generational patterns can go either way. Unfortunately, we tend to see the problematic ones far more often than the ones that work for good.

We all come from people whose blended customs were or were not handed down to us. One of my ancestors was a judge, and one was tossed from the Quakers for drinking whiskey. One was a Bible-thumper; another became a doctor at a time when few women could. One generation impacts the next. Traditions are cherished or chucked.

How many generations do you think influenced how you were raised?

Take another look at your chart—using either elements or keywords—and see if you can get a glimpse into the time and space that created you, your parents, or your grandparents. More on family patterns in chapter 5.

Moving into the Minors

Okay, time for a third card for the people on your chart.

By now, you've made a note of the Courts, suits, elements, and Majors for each person, checking for any patterns. If you made notes on what you've learned so far—you are writing in your journal, aren't you?—then go one step further.

For this exercise you'll need the Minor Arcana cards. If you want to use the whole deck instead of just the Minors, that's okay. Or if you want to use the Majors again, that's okay too. Who knows, your ancestor may have lived an archetypal life, so it makes sense if a Major Arcana card is one of your draws.

Start with each person in your chart and draw a Minor Arcana card. Right now, you want to get a sense of their everyday world. Again, I pulled one card and then returned it to the deck before drawing for another person. If you're unsure of the meaning of the number on the Minors, use this simple chart

1	2	3	4	5
beginnings, self	diplomatic partnership	creativity, celebration	structure, foundation	change, challenge
6	7	8	9	10
balance, peace	spiritual mastery	karma, choice	completion, humanitarian	new cycle, contentment

Now, be on the lookout for patterns. Is your family legacy filled with Swords? Does it have a preponderance of one or two numbers? When I added in the meaning of the numbers to my chart, I was shocked to see more threes than anything else. Threes are often the lightest and happiest of the numbers. That made me wonder if the family showed a happy face as their mask even though they might have been going through tough times. Hmmm.

Of the fourteen people on my chart, I only knew four, so it was fascinating to see if I could discern any family patterns that 1) came down to me through time and DNA, 2) gave me clues about why I'm me, or 3) help me find a way to communicate with a specific ancestor.

Of the fourteen people on my chart, my immediate family had the most Pentacles and the least Cups. Wands and Swords were well-balanced. Mom got the Six of Cups, and Dad the Ace of Pentacles.

This draw clarified a lot about my parents. I know Dad worked hard to make sure we were well-provided for. Mom, who had had a terrible childhood, spent the rest of her life making sure we all had good ones, confident in her never-wavering love. For her, the Six of Cups wasn't a happy childhood memory, but it was one that she wanted to create for us.

What can you learn by your draw? Are you seeing a balance of elements or numbers, e.g., lots of sixes or an abundance of Water cards (Cups)?

I'd love it if you'd take a few moments just to take in what you've learned about your immediate family. Does this help you understand something about yourself? And do you feel comfortable correlating cards with people?

If you want to do more of this exercise before moving on, draw Courts, Majors, and Minors for your siblings, aunts, uncles, or friends. Doing this exercise is a lot like taking a down and dirty look at someone's astrology chart, as in: "Oh, I see you have the Sun in Cancer in the fourth house," versus tarot saying "Oh, I see you wearing the mask of the Knight of Swords while battling the people in your work group, but your major life theme is the High Priestess. Hmmm, how does that work for you?"

SELECT AN ANCESTOR

Do you have one or more specific goals in working with your ancestors? Patterns you want to understand? Is there family karma that needs to be retired or healed? If there's an ancestor high on your list, this might be the one you really want to understand on as deep a level as possible.

Looking over everyone on your chart—again, no names are fine—pick someone you'd like to work with who is in Spirit. If everyone is still living, pick a relative who has passed away. Remember, this is just for practice.

In going over my own chart, I was tempted to pick one of the two Pages of Cups; one had the Lovers as a Major, the other had the Sun. So they looked like good candidates for an interesting discussion. But on second review, one of them had a Four of Swords as their "everyday life" card and the other had the Five of Cups. So, whoa, what was going on there? I'll put both on my high-priority list.

A second choice might be my mom's paternal side, as she didn't know the identity of her real father (Mr. G) until she was ninety years old. Just think of the things you knew about family while growing up. For me and those who are adopted, there's no knowledge of family stories, the black sheep, the immigration tales—all those things that help you understand your own lineage.

As I looked over my chart, I had to ask myself if I *wanted* to communicate with those ancestors of Mom's dad. Did I want to find out who they were and why her father never came forward? If it helped heal my anger, then absolutely.

Giving my chart one last look, I decided to choose Grandpa H., whose cards were the King of Wands, the Devil, and Two of Cups. Why that choice? Partly because I never knew him and partly because the idea of a King of Wands, the Devil, and the Two of Cups was intriguing. He was definitely a guy I'd want to meet.

Even more importantly, the stories I've heard about him sound as if he were a man who lived large, enjoyed life, and had a lot of fun. All those characteristics are a bit antithetical to mine, so maybe Gramps could help me start living life more as he did. He's my guy.

GETTING TO KNOW YOU SPREAD

With your chosen ancestor in mind, shuffle the deck and draw five cards and place them as shown on page 62. Note that the spread is in the form of a question mark—an appropriate design because it's about the person you want to know.

Card 1. How can I open the portal to communicate with this person?

Card 2. How does this person want to be present in my life?

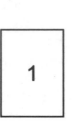

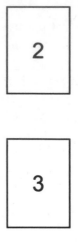

Card 3. How can I honor this person?

Card 4. What can I learn from this person?

Card 5. What message does this person have for me at this time?

Since this is a person you'll probably be working with in future exercises, be sure to journal the spread, the cards, and your thoughts.

ASTROLOGICAL CORRESPONDENCES

If you know the birth dates of anyone on your chart, compare their Sun sign with the Court card you drew for them. Dad was a Leo and yet I drew a Queen of Pentacles for him. What might that tell me?

I think Dad had a fiery (Leo) spirit—Wands—as after high school I know he jumped on a motorcycle and took off for Wyoming. But after he married and had kids, the need for financial stability closed in on the adventurous Lion. This is like marrying the Knight of Wands who turns into the King of Pentacles.

Mom, however, was a Sun sign Capricorn (Earth) with the Queen of Pentacles (Earth) as her card. She wanted stability. That was Mom. If you happen to know an ancestor's Moon or Rising sign, all the better.

Here's a chart to help you find the astrological element of your family member.

Element	Fire	Air	Water	Earth
Suit	Wands	Swords	Cups	Pentacles
Astrological correspondence	Aries, Leo, Sagittarius	Gemini, Libra, Aquarius	Cancer, Scorpio, Pisces	Taurus, Virgo, Capricorn

What if you don't know when an ancestor was born? Unless you've been climbing the family tree for a long time, you may not have that information. If you do, great. If you don't, just go with what you've already learned. Whatever information you get at this early stage is a step forward in doing Ancestral Tarot work.

Although the Court, Major, and Minor seem like a lot of information, they're just a small piece of what you'll be adding to your Whole Self Mandala in chapter 10.

AN ANCESTRAL MESSAGE

Now that you've had time to work with the cards and the elements, I want you to ask for a message from your mom and dad, your grandparents, or whichever ancestor you'd like to contact. Please choose someone who is in Spirit.

Take a few minutes just to create an energetic space into which you invite the ancestor. You might want to place an object in the center of your tarot reading cloth that is symbolic of the person from whom you want a message. For example, if I want to connect with my mother, I use a flat, round disk of garnet—Mom's birthstone.

For you, it may be a ring, a favorite watch, a tie, hat, or even a coffee cup.

I like lighting a candle to open a ritual for ancestral work. Then, I'll say a prayer, ask for a blessing, or purify with sage. You can find several suggestions for ritual work in chapter 11. If you can't burn sage inside where you live (I have a massively sensitive smoke detector, so burning can be a challenge, for example), you can purchase various botanical sprays. I use a black sage (*Salvia mellifera*) spray for cleansing both my area and my cards.

Whatever ritual you choose to use, remember the intent: to contact an ancestor using your tarot deck and to ask for a *meaningful message*.

For my draw, I asked for a message from my mom, my dad, and from them as a couple. If you have trouble connecting, call in your Spirit Guide and ask for help.

Which ancestor do you most want a message from at this time? Someone you recently lost, a distant ancestor, or someone in Spirit you did not get along with? Choose wisely.

Mom's message to me was the Nine of Cups. Before my mom crossed over, she told my siblings that the only person she worried about leaving was me. So I was thrilled to receive a message from her that told me to be happy and to celebrate life with all its quirks, turns, ups, and downs. Mom embraced humankind in every fashion. It's no surprise that her message was one of love and celebration.

I have to admit, Dad's was confusing. The tarot card that popped out for his message was the Four of Wands, typically called the marriage card. I don't think Dad is saying "go get married," but rather to get some friends together to celebrate a special occasion, or an achievement. Maybe like launching this book!?

Lastly, I drew one card as a message from Mom and Dad, the couple. The card I drew was the Three of Wands. Now this one was a surprise and actually threw me. The first thing I heard from both was "Nancy, your ship is coming in, and it's coming in really, really soon!" Now, I don't have a clue what ship they're referring to.

I did draw a clarifying card from an animal Oracle deck. I drew Hawk, the messenger. When I saw the card, the first thing I thought was "Those cheeky Faeries are at it again!" It was a confirmation that something was coming in (a ship/a message). As it turns out, Hawk is also one of my Spirit Guides.

ONE OF MANY PATTERNS

So far you've been looking at Majors, Minors, and Courts for a few people in your family tree. Now let's look at what ideas have been passed down the chain from grandparents to parents and then to you. The spread shown on page 66 is just the tip of the family pattern iceberg.

I am particularly fond of this spread because it can help you understand and begin to change unhealthy patterns that you may constantly repeat. This spread can help you get a handle on the legacy that steered you into making your choices. Use the whole deck.

Card 1. What pattern I inherited from the family

Card 2. What pattern my dad passed down to me

Card 3. What pattern my mom passed down to me

Card 4. What pattern dad's dad passed down to him

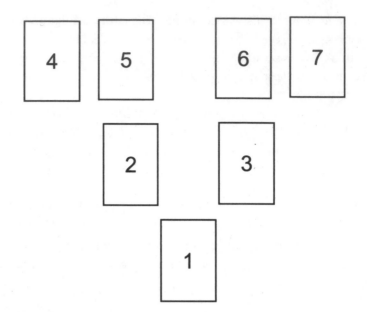

Card 5. What pattern dad's mom passed down to him

Card 6. What pattern mom's dad passed down to her

Card 7. What pattern mom's mom passed down to her

As you do this spread, you'll soon see that some patterns have faded while others are present in your life today. What if your mom inherited the pattern of the Five of Pentacles? Is this a pattern you can see in yourself today?

Again, don't look at each card as a stand-alone. Give yourself permission to consider all seven cards as one big picture. What story do they tell together?

Have you written all this in your journal?

So Far on Our Journey

You've learned:

- The number of your direct ancestors doubles with each generation.

- There are astrological correspondences to tarot suits and tarot cards.

- You've gained (hopefully) a richer picture of your mom and dad outside of their parental roles.

- You know a bit about the context in which a few of your ancestors lived.

- You worked with your first ancestor.

- You got your first ancestral message.

Journal Prompts

1 The thing that surprised me most about one of my ancestors was

_____ .

2. The ancestor I selected as to work with was _____

because _____

_____ .

3. The messages I received were _____

_____

_____ .

Sacred Tools: Gratitude

The first words out of my mouth every morning and the last at night are *Thank You*. I'm grateful for my life and my connection to Spirit. When I do ancestral work, I am sure to make my gratitude known—it's not something I really think about, it's just a part of how I do the work.

My guess is that you've seen a zillion gratitude journals around the Internet, especially over the last few years. These range from a five-minute journal to ones with prompts and blank pages. Some people write in a gratitude journal in the morning, some at night.

Did you know that a gratitude journal helps you feel better? "According to a study by researchers from the University of Minnesota and the University of Florida, having participants write down a list of positive events at the close of a day—and why the events made them happy—lowered their self-reported stress levels and gave them a greater sense of· calm at night," according to Huffington Post, July 8, 2015.

While I agree that a gratitude journal does help us realize how blessed our lives are, if you're going through difficult ancestral work, it's normal that your grief, sadness, or anger can make it hard to feel grateful. However, by adding bits and bobs of gratitude to your ancestral journal, healing begins its long journey.

And as you work with the ancestors, your gratitude may come in the form of thanks for healing, protection, understanding, or the fact that you're a living testament to their love.

Chapter 5

Ancestors of Blood

Ancestors of Blood are those with whom you share genetic material. Ancestral Tarot work takes one of two avenues: the one that leads to gratitude and the one that leads to healing.

You have your own reasons for connecting with ancestors, particularly those you knew. Some you loved and their passing left an empty space that feels unfillable. Others affected you in ways that were belittling, discounting, or downright abusive.

Whether you want to give thanks for their existence or heal your own, this is the chapter to begin that process. And as you work through the exercises, you may find that forgiveness itself becomes a third avenue—forgiveness for a loved one who left you, forgiveness of yourself for not being able to change that which you could not control.

WHAT'S IN YOUR LINEAGE?

We are all born into a family system from which we inherit a variety of traits, both positive and negative. Some are from nature (genetics), and some are from nurture (learned). The physical traits are the easy ones to spot. You have your dad's eyes and your mom's red hair. You have a heart-shaped birthmark just like Cousin Sue, and your dimples make you a dead ringer for Auntie Grace. You might as well enjoy those traits because, save for surgery, they're yours for life.

Nonphysical family traits, the nurture ones, aren't so easy to shed. They're the ones passed along from generation to generation via learned behavior. Some are ones we're lucky to have, like resilience, while others, such as domestic abuse, are not. By working with the ancestors, you can strengthen the traits that feed your soul and heal yourself of the ones that may have plagued your family for generations. My guess is that we all inherit both sides of the coin: good and bad.

Tip: As you begin ancestral work, you may want to concentrate on one side of the family or the other. Doing both sides works well if you're working within a family unit—i.e., mom, dad, kids. If the issues, whether good or not-so-good, are one-sided, then you may want to focus on that side first.

So let's start with looking at our inheritance.

Hand-Me-Down Spread

In this spread you'll find the traits handed down from both sides of the family along with the ancestral power that you've inherited. Once you draw a card for that power, you may think there's no way you inherited *this* from *your* family. Here's the deal: that power or those strengths may have skipped over your parents or grandparents, but they are yours, even though they may have come from generations ago.

Shuffle the entire deck and draw six cards, arranging them as shown on page 71.

Card 1. What traits have I inherited from my maternal (mother) line?

Card 2. What traits have I inherited from my paternal (father) line?

Card 3. How do my maternal line's traits help or hinder me?

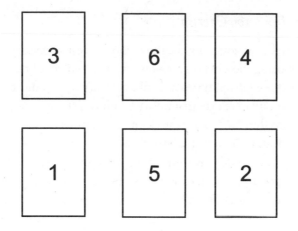

Card 4. How do my paternal line's traits help or hinder me?

Card 5. What is my blended ancestral power?

Card 6. Am I in alignment with my ancestral power?

Optional: If your sixth card shows that you are not in alignment with your blended ancestral power, draw a seventh card asking how to become aligned. If the seventh card doesn't answer your question, draw an eighth or a non-tarot card as a clarifier.

When I did this spread, I discovered my blended ancestral power was the Ace of Cups. (Didn't I draw that card earlier?) I feel as though I'm receiving a message about filling up my own soul's cup so that I will have plenty to share.

What cards did you draw? Did you need any clarifying cards? And, most importantly, are you in alignment with your ancestral power? If not, what was your seventh card? *Journal about the cards you drew, your thoughts about this spread, and whether it's changed how you see your family lines.*

The Family Traits You Cherish

If your family was emotionally healthy, your ancestral work will probably focus on honoring those who gave you life. This isn't confined to just your parents, but those tens of thousands of ancestors who stand behind you. I think it's important to realize that positive family dynamics didn't magically manifest out of thin air. They came from past family members who knew how to raise healthy, happy children.

As a kid you could have grown up in either a one- or two-parent home where good communication was standard. You learned early that healthy families show support and respect for one another and have clear-cut boundaries. Everyone in the family would have been valued and their feelings validated.

In this family, strong coping skills are passed down from parent to child or child to child. Time spent together as a family is important, as well as time spent in simply having fun. I don't know if you did this as a kid, but a favorite summertime activity for me was running through sprinklers, getting hosed down by Mom or Dad, or having the whole family cheer me on at a softball game. Fun wasn't kept under lock and key till vacation time, but was a part of everyday life.

If this were your family—or at least a big hunk of your family—losing part of the family to Mr. Death would have been heartbreaking.

If you've lost someone, you know that grief is not linear. It comes and goes in ways we cannot predetermine. Up one day, sobbing a week later—that's grief, particularly the grief that is new. Grief can flatten you like a pancake.

Ancestral Tarot won't remove your sense of loss, nor will it instantly heal you. But it can be used to honor, give thanks, and share gratitude to the one you loved. If yours was a loving relationship, you may just want to touch in to say "thank you," or "I miss you," or "Are you okay?"

If your family traits are ones that you want to continue, you might ask of the ancestors, "How can I honor the ancestor who initiated this pattern?"

or, "How can I continue this pattern for my highest good and the good of others?"

After my mom passed over, I had two questions:

1. Mom, are you okay?

2. Mom, will I see you again?

Tarot gave me answers that helped start the slow movement through grief: Judgement (Rebirth) and the Ace of Cups.

If you've lost someone recently and the grief feels unhealable, do the two-card spread asking the same questions as I did. You may want to ask more questions and draw more than two cards if the first two don't give you enough information. Grief is such a tough one. Be kind to yourself and know that these cards are just the beginning of the healing process.

The Family Traits You Don't Want to Continue

Although I can't presume to cover all inherited family traits, I do want to talk about some that are among the most prevalent.

There are so many problematic, hurtful dynamics that thrive in a dysfunctional family that it's important to call them out. Unhealthy relationships can be so insidious that you may have grown up in one without realizing it. Or you may realize it all too well. That's why you want to do healing work.

If you grew up in a dysfunctional family, it's likely that one or both of your parents grew up in that type of family too. There is a lot of generational healing that needs to be done. Now, I'm not a mental health professional, but I do want to briefly touch on some of the ways you may have been wounded in your youth or are still being wounded.

In a dysfunctional family, control is a biggie. It can manifest in so many ways, some of them blatant, others subtle. Instead of guiding you to making good, healthy decisions, decisions were made for you. This could manifest in telling you what you could wear or whether you could be friends with someone.

It's also possible that someone of authority in your family exerted control by withholding money, food, love, or affection. Other ways of controlling include the threat or actual use of physical, mental, or emotional violence. You may have been the family scapegoat, getting the blame for everything, or you could have been the older sibling who was forced to take care of younger brothers and sisters because of the death or absence of a parent.

You may have been criticized for not being perfect. Maybe you were locked out of your house or had a parent who was overly involved in your life or one who used you as a sledgehammer in arguments with a spouse or ex.

You may also have suffered from gaslighting. This is the practice of telling someone that what they saw or experienced wasn't real. Gaslighting makes you question your own sanity.

If any of these sound familiar, it's possible that you may have survived by withdrawing, socially isolating, suffering depression or anxiety, being self-critical, or acting out.

Dealing with Your Fear

If the idea of working with an ancestor who caused you trauma feels scary, that's because it is. If you're up for it, before reading further, draw four cards and let's see how you can do this work while still acknowledging that fear.

Card 1. Where is my fear manifesting in my life today?

Card 2. How does staying in this fear help me?

Card 3. How is this fear derailing my life?

Card 4. How can I safely face this fear?

The Fateful Five—Patterns that Need Breaking

Passive-Aggressiveness

While aggressive traits are right out there in the open for all to see, passive-aggressive ones are subtler. Instead of directly confronting an issue, the passive-aggressive person uses less obvious means to land a blow.

Actions can consist of behavior such as sulking, deliberately not following through on a request such as "forgetting" to pick up clothes at the cleaners, or making cruel comments couched in humor.

Is connecting with the ancestors to find the origin of this trait worth the time and effort? It is if you want to be the one person in the family who breaks that style of communication. As this is a learned behavior, if you don't try to heal the pattern, you can fall victim to it almost without realizing it. And the beat goes on.

Limiting Beliefs

If you grew up in a family where you always heard about the things you or the family can't do, you're a victim of limiting beliefs—"We can't afford

that," or "That's too dangerous," or "People are bad," or "No one in the family goes to college." These beliefs may impact you financially, emotionally, or in your worldview. Limiting beliefs turn a universe of opportunity into a tiny enclosure that keeps you as bound as the woman in the Eight of Swords.

Fortunately, like the woman in this card, you can walk away from the paralyzing thoughts (the swords) by stepping forward, wriggling out of those loosely bound ties, and removing the blindfold—*in other words, by working with the ancestors who originated those limiting beliefs.*

First, heal the damage done to you. Then discard this way of thinking.

One thing to consider is that one or more of these limiting beliefs may have been based on a real situation. For example, go back four or five generations and the family may have had a helluva financial struggle. In fact, they may have suffered to the point that every penny was the difference between life and death. Over time, though, the need to stringently conserve somehow evolved into the belief that there's never enough.

That Old Gremlin, Fear

I was meeting with a friend of mine, discussing the differences in growing up in my generation versus growing up as part of her millennial generation. I told her that the summer I was fifteen years old, I washed dishes on a ship cruising Alaska's Inside Passage. My friend said that her mother would never have let her do that, for fear that she would be murdered, kidnapped, or worse.

I realize that the times have changed, and young girls are more at risk than when I was growing up, but somewhere in her family is a fear that goes a step beyond—a fear that saw no solution other than saying, "No, you can't go!"

Who knows, this fear might have begun ten generations ago, caused by an attack on a young girl in the family or maybe a horrific incident while traveling.

In my own family there's a fear-based belief that something catastrophic will happen to someone we love if they aren't in our immediate vicinity. As I mentioned elsewhere in the book, my dad was an A+ worrier. He called home every day just to check that everyone was okay, and if one of us was sick, he called multiple times. That trait continues.

A Skewed Worldview

Is the world dangerous? Is everyone mean?

Some people see the world and everyone in it as one big lump of cancer-producing coal. Does that sound like how you were raised? If so, your family (and probably your ancestral) worldview is tilted about 45 degrees off-axis.

The challenge with this kind of worldview is the "all" or "everyone" philosophy. And the people who have that viewpoint tend to hang out with others of like mind. Doesn't it make you wonder if, ancestrally, they all shared a common experience that made their worlds such a big nasty place?

If this is your ancestral worldview and you're reading this book, chances are you've already broken that pattern. (Yeah!) But believe it or not, bits and bobs of this mindset could still be lingering, hiding out in plain sight.

How does that work? Think about it this way: You don't buy the "All Irish are drunks" mindset, but have you left behind the "Everyone on welfare is lazy" or "Homeless people brought it on themselves" patterns?

The familial issue here is in seeing individuals not for themselves but as part of a larger and more dangerous group. Something to consider, eh?

Tyrants (also known as "Never Question Me")

I have met many people who grew up in a home where one parent or the other was an absolute tyrant. If dinner wasn't on the table at 6 p.m., all hell broke loose. If your skirt was half an inch too short, you were grounded. Back talk an adult and buy yourself a ticket to your room or worse.

Let's go back to nature vs. nurture. Did the tyrant in your family learn this behavior during their own childhood? Probably, as I don't believe most of us are born to be bullies. In the tyrant, we're seeing the worst possible side of the Emperor (Major 4).

Family Pattern Spread

If your family inherited any of the Fateful Five or other unhealthy patterns, it's time to recognize them. Then, the healing process can begin.

For me, a family pattern that plays hell in the present is perfectionism, which is both a limiting belief and a skewed worldview. It can be a killer, because no matter what I do, it's not good enough.

To begin working with negative family patterns, use the entire deck and draw five cards.

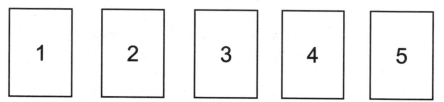

Card 1. What is the theme of the pattern? (This can be drawn from whole deck or Majors only.)

Card 2. Which ancestor was the pattern's originator?

Card 3. Why did this pattern begin?

Card 4. What is the *first step* I can take to begin breaking this pattern?

Card 5. What message do the ancestors have for me about this
   pattern?

The theme for me (Seven of Cups) is I can't make a choice because I'm
not sure the choice I make is going to be the *perfect* one. Well, that's just
great. What a crappy way to go through life!

The pattern originated with someone who felt they had to stand up
and fight for their values or their beliefs (Seven of Wands). And if that's the
case, then those values or those beliefs had damned well better be *perfect*.
I believe the pattern began with a married couple who were invested in
everything about their lives "looking" perfect, regardless of how imperfect
it might have been (The Lovers).

The key to breaking the pattern: old Mr. Death. To tell you the truth,
what I'm hearing him say is "It's over, let it go. Time to move on. Nothing is
going to be perfect, so let this one go." The ancestral message of Judgement
tells me that perfectionism is keeping me from creating and embracing a
new way of living.

But because I'm more into action than just saying "let it go," I wanted a
practical first step from my Death card. So I drew another card, asking for
a right action. I pulled the Ace of Cups. Someone once referred to this Ace
as the Holy Grail—that thing that most nourishes the soul. The message for
me? Drink a cup filled with what gives my heart and soul life.

For me, that Ace of Cups translates to working with the ancestors,
doing tarot, and writing. It's also about helping other people break the

chains of whatever is keeping them from being their best and most authentic self. I do not have to be perfect in my practice, but I do have to care.

Is it just me, or is the Ace of Cups coming up time and time again?

Tip: As you can probably tell, I'm not much for sticking to a spread if it doesn't give me all the information I need. I have zero issues with adding as many clarifying cards as needed in order to solve the problem or answer the question. Whether your clarifiers are crystals, runes, a pendulum, oracles, or tea leaves, don't hesitate to use them if the spread and the tarot cards you drew aren't giving you the info you need.

IS HEALING ALWAYS POSSIBLE?

In truth, family systems are a lot like weather patterns: one day a tornado hits, the next day a gentle rain announces spring, and the next a flood of epic proportions washes away your home. Family dynamics are ever-evolving. A father who loved you intensely throughout childhood may have become a tyrant or worse as you aged. A mother you adored may have passed over while you still desperately needed her. I know people who never knew if balmy weather or a tornado would be waiting behind the door when they got home from school.

When you begin working with Ancestral Tarot, you'll discover that there are some family members you don't care that much about working with—they're the family equivalent of the hurricane. Others will be a joy. Getting to the individual you end up working with isn't like spinning the Wheel of Fortune and—bam!—a random ancestor pops out. You'll find, fairly quickly, that you can easily pinpoint the ones you want to know better. You'll also discover the ones whose actions have brought you to this book.

You may have an ancestor who was so vile to you in life that you don't want to work with them in death. But you may want to understand why they were the way they were. You may also want to learn how to begin healing the wounds they inflicted on you. I hope you do.

However, you may also wonder if there are times when healing isn't possible. That's a great question and one I've thought a lot about. Can a Holocaust survivor truly heal from the soul-sucking inhumanity they experienced? Can a woman who was sold from person to person recover from her deep wounds? I hope the answer is at least a conditional yes. But I also recognize there may be some instances when the truthful response is no.

If you survived a situation where you don't see healing is ever going to be possible, I've been given permission by tarot deck creator Joanna Powell Colbert (*www.joannapowellcolbert.com*) to share this tarot spread with you. Although Joanna didn't realize it at the time, I think she created it especially for this book.

If Healing Can't Happen Spread

Use your entire deck for this seven-card spread. Design the spread layout in any way you desire.

Card 1. What breaks my heart? What am I grieving? What has been shattered during a Tower time? (If a positive card appears in this position, read its reversed or its shadow side.)

Card 2. What insight emerges as I sit with my grief?

Card 3. What inspiration and promise am I not seeing?

Card 4. When all hope is lost, what remains?

Card 5. What is the medicine—the gift—of my sacred wound?

Card 6. What wants to be remembered and restored?

Card 7. How might I be generous with the blessing of grace and hope?

WHEN FAMILY PATTERNS ARE REALLY GROUP PATTERNS

Let's face it, ancestral work is challenging enough without throwing in the misery, prejudice, persecution, and cruel treatment experienced if you belong to a group that isn't part of a cisgender, vanilla, Western European, Christian heritage.

All family dynamics—regardless of which group you belong to—are inherently problematic. (Remember my comment about storm systems?) In fact, when out for a drink with my blended race great-niece, our toast to each other was: "Here's to our fucked-up family." No joke, we all have them.

If you are gay, lesbian, bi, trans, African American, Jewish, Native American, Italian, Irish, Muslim, or any group that is or has been maligned or persecuted, your ancestral work is going to have a twist. That's because your family patterns go beyond the personal and become part of a group pattern. Let me give you an example.

If your Irish great-great-grandparents came to the United States in the late nineteenth century, they would have seen "No Irish Need Apply" signs in store windows. As you begin to work with your Irish ancestors, it's possible that you'll find at least one ancestor who, as a member of that group, originated a pattern of shame or, conversely, defiance toward authority. They could also have been the one who embraced a spirit of determination and resilience or the one who became the family's hell-raising alcoholic.

Do you have a sexual identification beyond heterosexual? Then you may be the first to break a family/group religious pattern of prejudice, intolerance, or ignorance. And members of just about any religious group outside of whatever was mainstream Western Christianity at the time most likely carry some family/group pattern of persecution: Jews in Eastern Europe during the pogroms, non-Catholics during the Spanish Inquisition, or Muslims in the post-9/11 United States.

As if basic ancestral work weren't hard enough . . .

So how do you do Ancestral Tarot when you're working with a family that either created or experienced group-size patterns? The first thing I recommend is a tarot reading based on the trauma/pattern of the group to which your ancestors—and possibly you—belonged. The reading is about helping you begin healing the inner child who suffered from this pattern. If you're in a minority, I'm pretty sure you don't need my help in identifying prejudice. And I'm also pretty sure that your little kid within carries a big wound.

Inner Child Healing Spread

 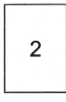

| 1 | 2 | 3 | 4 | 5 |

Card 1. How does my inner child feel right now?

Card 2. What family pattern scarred my inner child?

Card 3. What practical step can I take to begin healing my inner child?

Card 4. How can I protect my inner child from future harm?

Card 5. What message does my inner child have for me?

WHEN GROUP PATTERNS ARE GENERATIONAL

Has this ever happened to you? Your dad makes some kind of outrageous demand and when you question him, his response is "That's the way it is!" So of course you respond or not, depending on how invested Dad is in the demand. You comply or not, depending on the consequences. Dad is probably getting mad, and you're probably feeling that you're never heard.

If you've gone through this—and who hasn't?—you're experiencing the blowback of a generational pattern: "Grandpa did it this way, thus it is *the* way." I know you know what I'm talking about.

Generational patterns are fairly easy to recognize because they begin with a statement similar to "My dad did it this way," or "When I was a kid, we did it this way," or "If your grandmother were still alive, she would. . ."

Strangely enough, we all run around with generational patterns—even you and I. Yours may be the way you change your relationship status on Facebook. Mine may be how annoyed I get when someone minimizes my generation's angst. One generation complains about millennials, another about boomers.

Generational patterns aren't that big a deal—unless they are. The big deal ones are the kind that make you doubt your own instincts or make you feel bad about yourself, undervalue your experience, or leave you feeling like a dummy. If that's something you're dealing with, then absolutely, put it on the list for identifying the origin and working on healing the pain, and bring in tarot to help break the chains. Sometimes, all it takes is a willingness to be okay with being an outlier.

Healing from a Family Group or Generational Pattern Spread

```
┌─────┐ ┌─────┐ ┌─────┐ ┌─────┐ ┌─────┐
│  1  │ │  2  │ │  3  │ │  4  │ │  5  │
└─────┘ └─────┘ └─────┘ └─────┘ └─────┘
```

Card 1. How has this group or generational attitude impacted my life?

Card 2. What is the emotional weight of this intolerance?

Card 3. How has this belief affected how I see myself?

Card 4. How I can begin to heal from this experience?

Card 5. How can the ancestors help in this healing?

It's my hope that this spread will begin to give you more strength or an increased self-confidence. If not, you might want to draw either clarifier cards or, instead of one card per spread position, try three. If you've experienced prejudice, the pain can run deep.

Breaking the Pattern of Addiction

Because addiction is such an important topic, I didn't want to leave this chapter without addressing it. If you grew up in an addictive environment and are continuing that pattern, then the chances remain high that your children will following the same path. Sadly, one more generation of addicts is born.

Life doesn't have to be that way. *You* can be the one who breaks the pattern, not only for yourself, but for your kids and their kids. I know it's not easy being the one to work through a pattern like this, and in fact, you may be asking, "Why me?" I get it. You may even think your family pattern of addiction is benign, while the truth is it can keep you off-balance for a lifetime. One day everything looks fine, and the next all hell breaks loose.

Part of the pain with growing up with addicted parents or grandparents is suffering the grief over losing something that never was, such as a healthy relationship with the person who disappeared into their addiction.

Breaking the Addiction Pattern Spread

If addiction is a family pattern from which you want to heal, shuffle your entire deck and draw seven cards for the positions shown in the layout on page 86. Remember, you can always draw more cards if needed.

Card 1. How did the pattern of addiction begin?

Card 2. How is maintaining this pattern benefiting me?

Card 3. What has this pattern stolen from me?

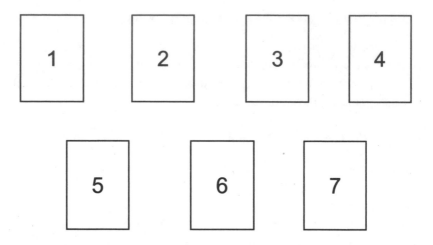

Card 4. What action can I take to break this pattern?

Card 5. How can I honor my ancestors who suffered with this pattern?

Card 6. How will breaking and healing this pattern benefit future family?

Card 7. What advice does my family Spirit Guide have about this issue?

Just checking . . . are you writing all of this down?

THE ANCIENT ONES

The last group of Ancestors of Blood to consider are the Ancient Ones. These are the ones who have contributed a tiny percentage of their DNA to you. I'm not talking about ancestors from 400 or 500 years ago, but the ones from thousands of years ago. In fact, your connection with them is more anthropological than genealogical. But they are still a member of the very long line of people who created you. They lived prerecorded history and the level of their connection to the living could be so slim as to be almost nonexistent.

You will never know their names, and you may never know where they lived, save for the fact that all of us genetically came out of Africa. When I psychically "see" the Ancient Ones, I only see wisps of Spirit, not even ghostlike, but more like a whisper.

When I first began working with the Ancient Ones, I thought their messages would be about survival, because that's pretty much what their lives were like. Find bear, chase bear, eat bear—or become bear's dinner.

Is there value in making this connection, even if it's only a onetime shot? For me the answer is a definite yes. That's because I want to know what message they may have for me—one that has drifted down through time—*and* I want to know how I can honor them.

I thought a lot about what I wanted to know from the Ancient Ones. And wouldn't you know it, they were as good at pulling the rug out from under my preconceived notions as the Faeries. Instead of sending messages about survival (Pentacles), nearly all the questions I asked were answered in the suit of Cups.

Try this Ancient Ones spread and see what comes up for you.

Ancient Ones Spread

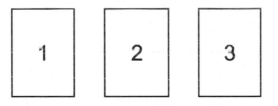

Card 1. How can I best communicate with the Ancient Ones?

Card 2. What message do the (collective) Ancient Ones have for me?

Card 3. How can I best honor those of my blood who lived
millennia before me?

When I did this spread, the cards told me that the best way for me to
communicate is with an open heart. In addition, I was told that every time
I do something Queen of Cup-ish, like volunteering, giving food to the
homeless, or helping someone who's in pain, *that* is their message.

As to how I could best honor them, I drew the Six of Cups. For those
with a difficult childhood this is not a terribly comforting card. But for
me it takes me back to my grandparents, the family stories and history I
learned when I was so young. I honor the Ancient Ones by remembering
them.

SAYING THANK YOU AND GOODBYE

As you end this chapter, you've either found first steps to healing or discovered how much gratitude you have for the ancestors. I know that Ancestors
of Blood can be the most challenging to engage with. Regardless of the reasons you came to this book, I hope that this spread gives you at least part
of what you were hoping for.

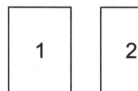 

Card 1. Which ancestor is with me on this journey?

Card 2. What message do you have for me?

Card 3. What lesson can I learn from your life?

Card 4. What strengths have I inherited from you?

Card 5. What can I do in my daily life to honor you?

Journal Prompts

1. What do I hope to accomplish working with the Ancestors of Blood?

   _____ .

2. Which ancestor do I want to connect to, and why?

   _____

3. Is there a specific family pattern I feel the ancestors can help me with?

   _____

4. Who in real life can support me if this work becomes too difficult?

   _____ .

5. Do I feel emotionally stable enough to work on this pattern?

   _____ .

6. If I break a generations-long family pattern, how will I feel?

   _____ .

If, at any point, your Ancestral Tarot work begins to overwhelm you or make you feel anxious or depressed, or it just seems too difficult, please consider work with a mental health professional.

Chapter 6

Ancestors of Place

A ncestors of Place are the ancestors who lived in your family's place of origin. They could have lived one hundred years or thousands of years ago.

If you worked through all the exercises in chapter 5, you have a lot to think and write about. But if you're ready to meet another type of ancestor, let's do it now.

Connecting with Ancestors of Place is—seriously—like coming home. Once you tap into those ancestors, you'll understand why you're so drawn to a specific town or country or why you innately know how to bake Irish soda bread or build a stone wall. These connections can open you up to a culture and customs you can embrace as your own, because they *are* yours.

Before jumping into this chapter, how about doing a one-card draw, asking only how best to connect with these ancestors. This will give you a jumping-off point for working with the ancestors in this chapter.

I feel pretty good about drawing the Three of Cups—the card of happiness, celebration, and gatherings. Funny, but what that one card tells me is that working with the Ancestors of Place will open me up to being more social, going to more events, teaching more, and going places with more people. What I'm also hearing is that working with this bunch of ancestors is going to prompt me to get out and have some fun. Ha! Does the Three of Cups realize it's talking to a Hierophant?

What if your one-card draw were the Tower or the Nine of Swords? What does this tell you? Is it scary to think about making this connection or does it pique your curiosity? I don't know which card you drew, but I'd really be interested in hearing about it. (Let me know at *sageandshadow @gmail.com*.)

Ancestors of Place are part of your family's genetic and cultural roots. They are the keepers of your ancestral practices as they relate to a specific site. They can help you discover the rituals, everyday practices, traditions, and even how they worked with *their* ancestors.

And in a sneaky way, those ancestral practices may have already popped up in your life. While you may think that the special entrée your mom served at Christmas was just something she found in a recipe book, the truth is it's one that your Ancestors of Place would have known well. Sadly, where it originated is lost in time. But why, you have to ask yourself, was your mom drawn to that particular recipe?

I know your family may or may not have passed down stories from many generations ago, but I promise that something in your life that you take for granted came to you from Ancestors of Place. It may be a color you're drawn to, food you like, a predisposition to being an incredible swimmer, or your attraction to mountain climbing.

Personally, I blame a few tiny specks of DNA for my love of pizza and Mexican food. Oh, that it were so . . . .

Whether your genetic home is the Great Steppe of Central Asia or the mountains of Snowdonia in northwestern Wales, you are connected to those ancestors. These are ones with whom you can work to learn how to honor the land where they were born and where their bones rest. Connect with these ancestors and you'll be connecting with your own cultural and genetic heritage.

Will you be proud of all your Ancestors of Place? No. In fact, some of them could be the progenitors of some pretty nasty family patterns. In my own work, however, I've found this to be rare. I think you will too.

One thing that's a little tricky, though, is that Ancestors of Place can be so merged with the Spirits of the Land that it's hard to separate the two. You'll find a spread for that in this chapter as well.

What's in a Name?

Before strapping on your time-travel goggles, let's first get a clue about where you are heading.

If your family immigrated to North America in what was known as the Great Wave of Immigration in the early twentieth century, you probably know which country they came from—unless, of course, your family wasn't the type to talk about the Old Country. For instance, life in Eastern Europe even pre-World War II was so difficult for Jews that even reminiscing about the town or village where they lived just wasn't a thing—too many bad memories.

If your family's immigration or migration was hundreds of years ago, you may be clueless about the places they came from. Most of my family lines were in the United States by the late 1600s, so finding their point of origin is a challenge.

Without doing a DNA test, is there any way to discover the land your ancestors called home? Yes, in fact there are a few.

First, ask your ancestors themselves. What can you learn from your tarot cards? Let me add here that this is an exercise that benefits from fewer cards and bigger chunks of your intuition.

Where Is My Homeland? Spread

Shuffle the entire deck and draw five to seven cards. Lay them out as shown on page 94. Next, look over the cards, not worrying about the meaning of each one, but rather the feel. Be listening for any voices you hear or messages emanating from your cards.

I drew:

The Cup cards bring a message that the place is probably one I've already visited. And based solely on intuition, I was there with someone I was close to in this life. It was an agrarian society that was totally connected with nature, including the movement of the heavens (the Star). I've gotta think about this one a little, although my gut says this was somewhere in Scotland.

If *your* gut is giving you a message about place, you can flip three cards looking for a yes/no answer, e.g., "Was this place in France?" If two of the three cards are upright, the answer is yes, if two are reversed, the answer is no.

If the yes/no method doesn't feel solid enough, try my third method. Here, you'll be using a free and sneaky feature on *Ancestry.com* that a lot of people don't know exists. Just Google "surname meaning ancestry" and a link from *Ancestry.com* will pop up.) I entered one of my family surnames (Snow) and got this result:

- *English: nickname denoting someone with very white hair or an exceptionally pale complexion, from Old English snaw "snow."*

If *Ancestry.com* has changed that page, GenealogyBank has one as well at *www.genealogybank.com* (click on "Surname Meaning" at the bottom of the page) although it doesn't have as many surnames in the database. You can also just Google "surname meanings" and you'll find other sites with basically the same information.

I wish I could tell you that finding a surname origin was the end of your search, but—joke's on us—surnames are relatively new compared to the history of humankind on Earth.

In Britain, for example, surnames weren't adopted until the twelfth or fourteenth centuries, and even then the practice wasn't universal. Surnames, as Western Europeans know them, came into being when the population in a given area grew to the point that a single name was no longer a sufficient identifier. As populations grew, surnames multiplied.

When introduced, surnames often referred to a geographical feature (Brooks, Rivers, Hill), a physical attribute (like white-haired Snow), a trade (Weaver), or any number of other factors. Throw into that mess the Scandinavian custom of patronymics deriving from a father's name and you'll be begging for a DNA test!

Of all the naming conventions, patronymics are probably the one that can really trip you up, as how they are formed changes depending on the country and culture. For instance, in Russia, "-vich" is a common naming convention, as in Ivan Nikolayevich (Ivan, son of Nikolay). In Nordic countries the surname was generated by using the ending "-son" or "-sen" to indicate "son of," or "-dotter/dottir/datter" for "daughter of." On top of that, there's the custom of giving a person a surname based on their father's first name. So, John, son of Peter Andres, becomes John Petersen. Confusing, I know.

If you want to dig into your surname a bit more, *Ancestry.com* also has a free message board system with more than twenty-five million posts. Here, you can search for any surname and find other users' comments and histories.

Not only can you look up your own surname, you can also look up the surnames for the ancestors that you already know, e.g., your grandmother's maiden name.

PLACES HAVE ENERGY

In my experience, it can be hard to untangle ancestral energy from the Spirits of the Land. With or without human footprints, all places have an energy. There are sacred places around the world that have been worshipped at for millennia. Go to one of them and the energy practically lifts you out of your shoes.

There are also places in the United States, especially places where the Ancestral Puebloans lived, that have an energy unlike any I've experienced elsewhere. Among them is a certain ruin on a hilltop close to the Grand Canyon. The energy there is so peaceful and yet strong (very Emperor-ish) that when sitting there amid the fallen walls, I feel as though I've entered another dimension.

These "homelands" are places the ancestors lived, where they married, had children, fought with warring elements, and eventually died. Ancestors of Place, especially those further back in history, were far closer to the land than most of us, so they would have easily recognized and worked with the magic of place.

Depending on your country of origin, your ancestors would have been familiar with nonhuman entities such as the Thunderbird whose flapping wings caused the wind to blow among peals of thunder. The Aos Sí was a fairylike race that your Irish ancestors would have left offerings for, in hopes of not giving offense. The *Huldufólk* of Iceland live in nature, but in a universe parallel to our own.

For us, connecting with Ancestors of Place gives us the added opportunity to identify, understand, and use the magic of our own ancestors as well as the magic of where they lived. Think of tapping into your Irish ancestors' knowledge of the stars, or your Greek ancestors' ability to build magnificent temples. Better still, your Viking forebearers' ability to navigate the oceans. Compared to how well the Ancestors of Place were connected to natural spirits, we're all a bit like orphans.

Once you discover your own Ancestors of Place, do some research into the beliefs, customs, and culture of where they lived. What a wonderful way to honor the ancestors by incorporating part of their spiritual beliefs into your own ancestral or magical rituals.

As you begin working with this group of ancestors, separating them from the Spirits of the Land can be challenging simply because they were *of* the land. We urban dwellers can be so disconnected from land energies even when it comes to the ground under our own homes. Do you honor the Spirits of the Land in a way your ancestors did? My guess is probably not. But that doesn't stop you from beginning to work with the land spirits at the same time you do the ancestors.

Try this simple three-card spread to learn more about your ancestor-land connection.

Ancestors of Place and Spirit of the Land Spread

Draw three cards for the Ancestors of Place, but first have a place in mind that you either know your family originated from or you intuited from your earlier tarot spread. Under these first three cards for the ancestors, place three more for the Spirits of that Land. Draw one more card to fill the gap between these rows: this is the Bridge card—the one that allows you to understand and work with both energies. The cards I drew are shown on page 98.

My quick two-sentence overview: I chose my Scottish ancestors, and at a glance, I'd say they were creative, frugal, and had large extended family units. The Spirits of the Land loved how the ancestors embraced them, handing down rituals from generation to generation. That Two of Swords tells me that I can't really pull the two energies apart.

When you did this spread, what were your cards? Did you understand the Bridge card or did you need to pull another card for clarification?

Once you've drawn these seven cards, do you feel that you'd like to go deeper into those particular ancestors and/or do you want to work with the

Spirits of the Land? For me, the two are so merged that if I work with one, I'm also working with the other.

Maybe it's just me, but I do want to learn about the nonhumans who inhabited the same place as my human ancestors. I feel called to include something about them in an honoring ritual. Right now, I'm drawn to the Scottish legend of the selkies—those who could change from seal to human by shedding their skin. I'll draw a card asking how best to incorporate the selkies into my ritual.

How to Find Ancestors of Place Using DNA

DNA testing has been available for years. It was originally used to prove or disprove paternity or help in solving crimes. But around the year 2000, the notion that DNA could be used to let people connect with other family members seemingly popped out of nowhere.

Using DNA, you can connect with living (and often unknown) relatives, find natural birth parents, and discover where your bloodline likely originated. This last is known as your genetic ethnicity.

Each DNA company has its own method of calculating ethnicity. That's why, if you do DNA testing at more than one company, you're going to see slightly different results. While one company may show you as 12 percent Scandinavian, another may say only 4 percent, or instead of broadly Scandinavian it may show that your DNA is from Sweden.

Ancestry.com is currently the largest DNA testing company, with more than sixteen million people tested, and counting. The advantage of a large database like this one is that it will improve your chances of finding other family members—particularly important if you were adopted. If you just want to know your genetic ethnicity, then the number of people in the database isn't as important.

In my own family, we've used DNA three times to discover a birth parent, as in all three instances, the biological father was unknown. After DNA testing and then communicating with other people who shared the same DNA results, we were able to pull the blanket off some old secrets.

This brings me to an important point. Your DNA results may contain information that you aren't emotionally prepared to receive. For example, you may discover that the man you consider your father is not actually your biological parent. Or perhaps you will learn that you belong to an unexpected ethnic group, possibly one that you have harbored prejudices against.

If, in fact, your DNA test reveals one whopper of a surprise, you're left with little recourse other than to come to grips with the who or why. What better use for tarot than that scenario?

Of the dozens of DNA test results I've seen, I can say this above all: *If you're not willing to be surprised, don't take the test.*

Having said that, though, I'm hoping that using DNA as a tool to connect with your ancestors outweighs the potential perils.

If you're interested in being tested, as I write, major companies include:

- *23andMe.com*

- *Ancestry.com*

- *MyHeritage.com*

- *criGenetics.com*

- *FamilyTreeDNA.com*

If you want to do actual family tree research, I'd recommend *Ancestry.com* as it has the largest DNA database of all the services and millions of historical records. The more people who take the test, the better your chances of finding a match and learning about your family tree.

23andMe.com is simple to use with easily understandable results. If your primary goal in doing DNA is to nail down your ancestry without getting into family tree research, this is the company for you. *CriGenetics.com* has more recently entered the DNA space. Its claim is the ability to take you *waaaaay* back in time genetically. The results will even tell you your maternal haplogroup. This is the group of genes that indicates your "original" parentage. Mine is K1a3, which originated in Neolithic Anatolia (what is now modern Turkey). What I find most interesting is that there's also a DNA percentage in the Iberian Peninsula, a place I've always been drawn to. Likewise I have a hint of ancient Peruvian DNA, and weirdly Machu Picchu has been on my bucket list since I was a kid. *Hmm . . .*

For now, DNA is not yet so exact as to place your family in a specific village, but as time goes on, it is getting more and more precise. That's probably due to a lot of DNA being extracted from the long-dead. Every single day I see articles about ancient remains being found under a new construction site or parking lot. Over time, DNA will get a lot better at zeroing in on your ancestral lands.

In case DNA testing interests you, prices vary among the companies, partly dependent on whether you want a health analysis along with your ethnic heritage—that typically adds another $50 or so. Want to get tested but want to save money? Check each of the companies around a holiday as most have big sales promotions over holiday weekends.

DNA and Your Ancestral Heritage

It would be nice if all our DNA came down the line in a neat bundle from ancestors who lived in prehistoric times or even several hundred years ago. Unfortunately, that's not how DNA works.

If you take a DNA test and your three siblings take the same test, none of your results will look exactly like the others. That's because you don't inherit a nice, neat long line of all your DNA—you inherit chunks.

Because your brother inherited a different chunk than you did doesn't mean you're not siblings. It just means that in the toss of the dice the two of you received different chunks or different percentages of a chunk. I have absolutely no proof, and this might be another book topic, but I'm not so sure that those chunks are random.

My DNA shows a tiny percentage of Native American and Ashkenazi Jewish. My sister's does not. My brother's DNA offers a 30 percent chunk from Ireland and Scotland; mine was 20 percent.

Remember, the percentage of any ethnicity is going to vary by testing service, but most results will place your heritage in the correct countries or locales. As test results improve, your ethnic place of origin will become more defined. My "broadly UK" is now starting to break down into London, Glasgow, and County Dublin.

If your heritage is Ashkenazi Jewish and your family consistently married within that Jewish community, it's not unlikely that your heritage results may be up to 99 percent European Jewish. Even then, testing can place your heritage within a geographic zone as specific as Eastern Romania, Western Ukraine, Moldova, Poland, and Moravia.

If you are of African descent, testing can bring back results as specific as Senegal River Valley, Niger, or Cameroon. Don't be surprised if all your African countries of origin are along Africa's west coast, once known as the Slave Coast. This is the area where Africans were most often kidnapped before being transported to the Caribbean or the Americas. However, even before the transatlantic slave trade, the mid-fifteenth century saw enslaved Africans being sold across Europe.

One last caveat about DNA testing. As you've probably seen in recent news, DNA has been used to catch people who committed horrific crimes in the past. How law enforcement uses DNA is controversial, even within the DNA community. Additionally, some people aren't comfortable with their DNA being stored at some facility. If these are concerns, carefully read the terms of service at whatever testing company you choose.

FAMILY LORE

I don't know a family that hasn't passed along tall tales and other lore about the past. Do any of these sound familiar?

- We're descended from an Indian princess.

- Our family comes from a long line of British royalty.

- Great-grandpa came to America from China.

- Our family came over on the *Mayflower*.

- Our ancestors died during the Spanish Inquisition.

With a few exceptions—the Indian princess being one—most family lore is based in truth, however slim that truth might be. The details may be wrong, but there is almost always a grain of truth somewhere in the story.

Although not as exact as DNA testing, you can use family tales to pinpoint, or at least get in the ballpark, in terms of your ethnicity. If the lore is about the *Mayflower*—a fact easy enough to check—even if the family wasn't on the ship, it's reasonable to conclude that they were living in England.

If you choose to follow this family lore method, you'll have to do more digging than using DNA and surnames, but it is an option.

WHERE TO BEGIN SPREAD

Using your entire deck, shuffle well and draw three cards. The questions to ask are:

Card 1. How can I best connect to Ancestors of Place using my surname as a clue?

Card 2. If I use DNA testing, how can I expect to benefit in my ancestral work?

Card 3. What message do my Ancestors of Place have for me as I begin this journey?

It's interesting that I drew the Moon for Card 1 (using my surname) as I'm certain that way back when, the family changed the surname from Hendricks to Hendrickson. The Moon, to me, bears that out as it is a card of hidden mysteries. I have benefited from DNA testing and my ships have already come in. I like that the message from Ancestors of Place is the Three of Pentacles—one of my favorite cards. The message I hear is that as I begin the journey with the Ancestors of Place, I will be meeting those whose hearts were anchored in creation.

ETHNICITY AND YOUR ANCESTORS

Once you track down your genetic origins, you're ready to begin your Ancestral Tarot work. Where you start depends on your goal. For me, working with Ancestors of Place helps me locate a region that's in my genetic code. That, then, will help me in working with the ancestors as well as the Spirits of the Land.

Although I live in a large city, I connect every day with the land spirits. I want to know how to connect with those ancestral land spirits as well. Who better to guide me in that than my Ancestors of Place?

You may want to connect with Ancestors of Place because you don't feel a connection to any single area. If you're adopted, connecting with this group of ancestors may help you feel that you *do have a place in this world* to which you belong. For you, identifying those ancestors can aid you in finding a home. Or your goal may be as simple as connecting to let the ancestors know that you're here and that you honor them.

TIMING AND ANCESTORS OF PLACE

Ancestors aren't sitting around waiting for your call. In this exercise you're going to use your tarot deck and discover the best time to make a connection with an Ancestor of Place. A full tarot deck is needed; a pendulum is optional.

Exercise

1. Picture the ancestor with whom you want to connect. Clearly, it's impossible for photos of most of your ancestors to exist, but picture that ancestor in your mind. I'm seeing an elderly Scottish woman sitting by a fireplace knitting socks. (Don't ask me where that came from. I don't have a clue.)

2. Choose a tarot card that you feel represents that ancestor. For me, I went to Wikipedia to find out what this woman might have looked like, or worn, or what everyday life might have been for her. I encourage you to do the same. I choose the Four of Pentacles. Leave your card in the deck.

3. Shuffle your deck and then cut it to create four piles. Don't worry if one pile is big and another tiny—sometimes it just works that way.

4. Look through each pile until you find the card you picked for the ancestor. Don't change the order of the cards in the piles.

5. Turn over the top card of the pile where you found your ancestral card.

6. The top card will tell you when it's easiest to connect with that ancestor. Of course, you can try to connect at any time; this timing card tells you when the opportunity to open the portal will be easiest.

Here's a simple chart you can use to calculate timing using the Minor Arcana. The Golden Dawn has a far more complex system, but this one works too.

Wands	Cups	Swords	Pontacles
Spring	Summer	Fall	Winter
Days	Weeks	Months	One Year

My timing card was a Cup card. Using the chart, this tells me that I'll be most successful approaching her in summertime. Since summer runs from the June solstice to the September equinox, I'll have a three-month window of opportunity.

If I want a more defined date, I would draw one card for each week of summer. You should be able to tell, based on which tarot cards were drawn, which week is best for you. Optionally, you can lay out cards for each week of summer and then, using your pendulum, let it help you decide on a week. Lastly, you could use the yes/no approach to pin down the best week.

Let me toss in one more thing. Timing is interpreted differently depending on which method you use. The Golden Dawn system is far more precisely laid out, giving specific dates for each tarot card.

What Do You Know about Place?

Let's say your genetic ethnicity places your distant ancestors in France. What do you know about this region during the era in which your ancestor may have lived? If you don't have a sense of what period of time the ancestor lived in, you can create your own system. For example, using the Major Arcana, randomly assign one card for each century, then do a draw and see which Major appears.

Also, use Wikipedia or a Google search, looking for what would have been the cultural norms including clothing, food, religion, burial customs, or ancestral worship. Look, too, for beliefs or customs, like how your Jewish ancestors were treated as opposed to your Catholic ones. Or what specific customs did the Ancestors of Place practice following a funeral?

In the following exercise, I'm asking you to embrace the gift from one of your Ancestors of Place. Discover how their knowledge can help you in your life today.

In truth, you may never find an ancestor's name in a history book, you may never know if the family came from West Wales or North Wales, and you may never know a single fact about them.

But what you do know is the place.

GIFT FROM THE ANCESTORS OF PLACE SPREAD

For this exercise, you'll need your full tarot deck. If possible, add to your reading space a plant or stone or photo or something symbolic of the Ancestor of Place you've chosen. One woman I know picked a small pyramid for her altar, another a photo of the Eiffel Tower.

After you've set up your space, take a few deep breaths until you feel grounded in your physical body. Then, picture the ancestor living in their original place. Next, draw three cards, placed as in this spread.

<table>
<tr><td>

1

</td><td>

3

</td><td>

2

</td></tr>
</table>

Card 1. The gift given to me by the spirit of that ancestor

Card 2. The gift given to me by the spirit of the place

Card 3. How I can best use the gifts in my life today?

I worked with my Scottish granny ancestor and drew these three cards:

Do you know what I considered the most interesting thing for me to understand? That the message from both the Ancestor and the Place was about love. It's not a surprise that they are interwoven via Death. Death tells me that the best way I can use those gifts of love is by working with those who have passed over. (I'm hearing a recurrent theme here.)

Journal Prompts

1. What I learned from this Ancestor of Place was

_____

_____ .

2. I asked the Ancestor of Place for a message. It is

_____

_____ .

3. I asked the Ancestor of Place if there are specific ways to honor them. The message was _____

_____

_____ .

Sacred Tools: A Personal Devotion

Ancestral work isn't about flipping a few cards and then moving on to some other metaphysical practice. The ancestors were real people who (mostly) want to work with you, and that work deserves some measure of your devotion.

Although you may want to develop a personal devotion at various phases of your ancestral work, for now let's create one that's a commitment or a dedication to the ancestors. Using your whole tarot deck, draw one card, asking for a foundation upon which to build your personal and private devotion to the ancestors.

As I drew the Seven of Pentacles, my devotion might be based around the concepts inherent in that card: thankfulness for my devotion to my work, for the seeds of ideas that the ancestors have helped plant, and for the strength to continue keeping watch over my ideas as they grow and flourish.

I would also add something about my promise to make my ancestors proud of the work I do and how much I want to leave a lineage that honors both them and me.

Chapter 7

Ancestors of Time

A ncestors of Time are those from past incarnations. This chapter is probably the one that's been the hardest to pin down, simply because Ancestors of Time encompass such a hodgepodge of people. These ancestors are the ones you had in other incarnations. That means you could be working with people from your last incarnation or one you lived hundreds or thousands of years ago.

That said, connecting with these ancestors can be just as important as connecting with Ancestors of Blood because the many lifetimes before this one continue to impact each of us today. I know mine do.

Are the patterns of another life following you in order to be healed, honored, or released? Or are they emerging so you can understand why you are drawn to or repelled by certain people in this lifetime?

WHO ARE ANCESTORS OF TIME?

Ancestors of Time are a fascinating conglomeration of people. They can be *you* in another incarnation, or they can be the people who knew you in a previous lifetime, or they could be your ancestors from a previous lifetime.

I believe we've all lived many lives, and thus, we have ancestors from those lives. If you think about the fact that you have more than one million direct ancestors in the last twenty generations of *this* life, just imagine how many you must have from previous lives. Overwhelming, huh?

Most of us have had inklings of other lives—if not direct evidence—so connecting with ancestors of past incarnations can answer some questions about personal or family patterns and possibly generate new ones.

I had an interesting experience several years ago. A close friend and I wanted to know if we had shared a past life. We underwent a joint past life regression, and upon being brought back to the present, we independently wrote down what we had experienced. When we compared notes, we were surprised/not surprised that the regression had taken us to the same lifetime.

In the regression we were both Native Americans who lived somewhere around the Great Lakes. She was a medicine man, I was his pupil. In my regression I saw that one of her hands was dark; in hers, she saw the same hand as being burned. The similarities in our experiences were mind-boggling. And, without getting into all the details, what I can say is that it explained the closeness of our friendship.

If you ever get a chance to do a regression with a friend or family member, it could change how you feel about past lives as well as how you relate to the people close to you.

The Ancestors of Time, as we know them, lived through momentous and personal life-changing events, both positive and negative. By connecting with these ancestors you might just find the original bad guy or good guy whose karma you're living out today.

Ancestors of Time can be personal ancestors, or they can be part of a generational or experiential collective you were part of. This kind of messes with your mind, doesn't it? Who knows if the family patterns or karma came from Ancestors of Blood, Place, or Time?

This is another one of those tricky things. Once you start doing tarot spreads for Ancestors of Time, try to focus on whether you're asking the *you* of another incarnation, an ancestor of the *you* in another incarnation, or an ancestor of *you* now but who was also an ancestor of *you* then.

I know, it's like one of those weird paradoxes that you can't wrap your head around.

ANCESTORS OF ANOTHER INCARNATION

Let's start with investigating the ancestors of you in another incarnation. If you can uncover what those ancestors went through during a lifetime, you may have a better understanding of the karma running down to the present day.

A quick note about karma: I'm pretty sure thousands of books have been written about karma, but for me, it just means this: Something you did in another life is playing out in this life. It functions like cause and effect. Let's say that you were the child of an Irish immigrant, coming to the United States in the mid-1840s. Your Irish ancestors probably worked the land until the famous Potato Famine, which sent tens of thousands to America.

As a result of that Irish lifetime, a pattern may have developed from that family that runs to your family today. Maybe you hate potatoes. Or maybe you work for humane immigration policies, collect Belleek china, have an underlying dislike of government, carry a limiting belief around food and money, or hold an expectation that life is going to be tough.

Exercise

Before moving on, go back to chapter 1 and the Which Ancestors Do I Want to Work With? spread. What card did you draw for Ancestors of Time? Grab your deck and toss a few cards just to see if this is still a group of ancestors you feel would be of benefit to work with. What card did you draw for working with Ancestors of Time? Next, what card did you draw for this question: What impact will working with this type of ancestor have on my life?

My two cards were The Chariot and The Sun.

What were yours?

Both my cards were from the Major Arcana, which most tarot readers believe carries greater significance than the Minor Arcana, and so I knew that working with this group of ancestors was going to be particularly meaningful

for me. Plus, with the Sun as the impact card, it looks as though the Ancestors of Time have some joyous living they want to introduce me to.

Is it always like this? Are you always going to draw "good" cards? Absolutely not. I just lucked into working with a lifetime that was filled with energy—especially that of living life large.

At this point, I want you to just stop and skim back over the notes you've taken in this book so far. Are you getting similar messages? I have to say that I keep hearing a "lighten up" theme in a lot of my cards.

If similar cards or similar themes keep appearing for you, what are they and what's the underlying message?

You're still journaling all of this, right?

Working with Your Personal Ancestors of Time

Let me show you one way I work with the personal Ancestors of Time, and then we'll do a spread for your chosen incarnation. As you'll see, this takes at least a sense of that lifetime as well as some research.

As I told you earlier, I'm drawn to the Little Bighorn Battlefield. I've gone there over and over—even though the Montana location is far from my California home. Why do I feel so happy there? Is it because all my friends from that life are buried there as soldiers, or is it because my friends from that lifetime won a battle there as Native Americans? Let's see if tarot can help me untangle that lifetime.

I also would like to know if there's some pattern I've carried forward from then, any messages my old-time friends have to share, or why I keep being pulled back there.

It's obvious, from those few questions, that this spread is going to be a flex spread. That means I can add or delete questions, add clarifying cards, and add more cards if the original card draw didn't give me sufficient information.

Another Lifetime Spread

Let's start out with the simple questions.

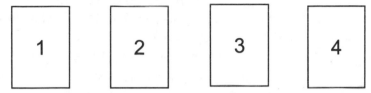

Card 1. Who was I in that lifetime?

Card 2. What pattern (if any) have I carried forward from then to now?

Card 3. What message do my old friends have for me?

Card 4. Why do I keep going back?

I'm going to admit it right now. I was totally shocked at these cards. When I saw the Hanged Man, I knew the me in that lifetime had to be a soldier. Why do I think that? Because I'm so drawn there, I've read multiple books about the period. In fact, if you checked out my bookcase right now, you'd see several shelves devoted to the Indian Wars (1876–1879).

Hang in there through the next paragraph—I'm telling you this story so you can find the story that helps unravel your own past incarnation.

One of the most significant events prior to the battle at Little Bighorn was a Sun Dance. The short version of this is that the Hunkpapa Lakota medicine man Sitting Bull had a vision of "soldiers falling into camp" (falling upside down). Based on that image, he knew that the soldiers were going to be defeated. So you'll understand when I saw the Hanged Man, I immediately knew I was a soldier falling into camp.

I was sorry to see that the Five of Pentacles still lives on from that lifetime. It's not really so much about being without, but it's more about the *fear* of being without (limiting belief). The Queen of Cups was a lovely message of love and nurturing from my old pals. As to why I keep returning? The Seven of Cups tells me I'm looking for something that was lost there. I think it is a sense of camaraderie—friendships that go far beyond the main.

Please note your cards and your thoughts about this specific incarnation, and relate it to a personal experience from today.

If you've never had a sense of another lifetime, draw four cards and let the images lead you into your own journey of discovery. Again, this requires you to read the cards a bit and trust your intuition a bit—it's a balancing act.

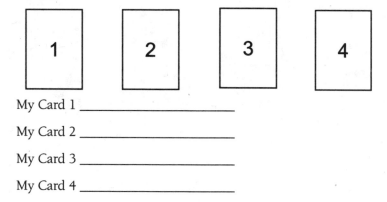

My Card 1 _____

My Card 2 _____

My Card 3 _____

My Card 4 _____

How might these cards guide you to another life? If you receive a Major Arcana, it will tell you something about the theme of that life. Personality will be evident if you draw a Court card. Everyday life will show in the Minors. It's possible to get multiples of each type of card.

The life I tapped into was _____.

My sample: These are the four cards I drew. My question before shuffling and drawing was: *I would like to be aware of a previously unknown lifetime that impacts my life today.*

Almost immediately I heard that it was a lifetime of building something sacred, like the High Priestess's temple. It took a lot of time (Knight of Pentacles), was incredibly difficult work (Ten of Wands), but the completion was a celebration to end all celebrations (Three of Cups). But the celebration went far beyond completing a task—emotionally it was the culmination of a lifetime of work done with love.

Draw a final card, asking: How does this life impact my life today?

The card I drew was Death. *And this is where I become way more vulnerable than I'm comfortable with.* I believe the level of sustained hard work in that other lifetime ended up killing me. As Death was my impact card, the message I hear is that committing to that level of sustained, dedicated work today is scary for me. The memory of it killing me remains.

Of course, you know what I'm going to do next. Yep, draw cards to determine exactly how I can release that memory.

If you're dealing with something like this as well, make sure you don't leave it at the aha moment. Move into the "how do I heal from this?" part to get the full benefit of this new insight.

Once you've completed this exercise, if there's another lifetime you'd like to explore, go ahead and do the draw, making sure you journal the results. Do this for as many lifetime experiences as you'd like.

Working with Ancestors of a Collective Experience

I'm going to assume that in one of your incarnations you belonged to a group that perished at the same time or close to the same time. When might this be?

It's possible that you perished during the Spanish flu pandemic that ravaged the world, at its worst in 1918. It's been estimated that between twenty and fifty million people died worldwide. The flu was so deadly that, in the United States, many towns and cities prohibited public gatherings at places such as churches or schools. Astonishingly, in one year, the life expectancy of Americans dropped by twelve years.

If you think this was your fate and you'd like to know more, pick up Gina Kolata's book *Flu* (Touchstone, 2001). It states that if a similar virus were to strike today, it would kill more people in a single year than heart disease, cancers, strokes, chronic pulmonary disease, AIDS, and Alzheimer's disease combined. Whether it's a coincidence or serendipity, as this book was being edited, we were in the midst of a 1918-type experience with COVID-19. How this plays out over the next year or so remains to be seen.

Another of your collective incarnations might be as a passenger on the *Titanic* or someone who celebrated the hundredth anniversary of the United States in 1876. Alternately, is it possible you witnessed the Great Fire of London in 1666, when one-third of the city was destroyed? Or perhaps you were among those forced to leave Spain as part of the attempt to purge that nation of all who weren't Roman Catholic. Could you have been one of the millions kidnapped from Africa and sold into slavery? None of these are mutually exclusive. Depending on the number of your past lives, you may have shared in many of these experiences.

One way to discover if you were a member of one of the groups who collectively experienced a life-altering event is to use your tarot deck. Can you draw cards that give you some sense of a group experience from a previous incarnation? Let's see.

A Collective Life Exercise

For this exercise, draw as many cards as you'd like from the whole deck. Is there any pattern or symbols that lead you to a specific lifetime?

Now again, this is where your intuition needs to come into play.

I drew: Page of Pentacles, Page of Cups, Sun, Empress, Star, Eight of Wands, Seven of Cups. What I "heard" was that my sister and I both drowned in a Great Flood. (I told you you'd need to trust your intuition.) This could be anything from dikes bursting in Holland to the Great Flood of 1844, to any number of hurricanes, typhoons, or tsunamis that killed thousands. I have no idea. But I will be drawing more cards to investigate the when and where. More importantly, I want to know what continues from that life to this.

You may approach this differently. It's possible that you already have a sense of that collective experience lifetime based on the things you've been drawn to. I know a woman who could not read enough about the *Titanic* sinking. No matter how many books she read or documentaries she saw, she had an obsessive need to learn more. For my money, she died on that ship.

If you feel more comfortable with a structured spread, here's one that can help you break one of those patterns of a group trauma.

We're in This Together Spread

I chose an *X* shape for the spread because I wanted to give an energy boost to the breaking away energy. It's time to leave behind those destructive group traumas or patterns you've been carrying around.

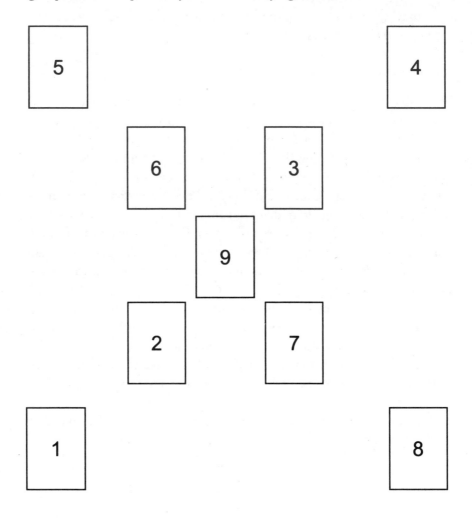

Card 1. How is this group trauma playing out in my life?

Card 2. What is the shadow keeping me from recovering?

Card 3. What is this shadow keeping me from experiencing in this life?

Card 4. What is the emotional cost of this trauma?

Card 5. What are my unresolved issues of this group pattern?

Card 6. How do I begin to move away from this group trauma/pattern?

Card 7. What ancestor is with me on this journey?

Card 8. How can this ancestor help with this trauma?

Card 9. How can my life change by healing this group trauma?

Remember: If you're having trouble interpreting any of the cards given their position in the spread, draw additional cards (either tarot or Oracle) for clarification.

For example if you drew the Hanged Man in position 6 (how to begin moving away from group trauma), you may be scratching your head. This is a great time to pull a clarifier from another deck, an Oracle, or from runes. What you'll be looking for, in a case like that, is an *action card* for the Hanged Man so when the time comes for him to climb down from that tree, you'll have a practical plan of action.

The cards I drew are shown on page 122.

How would you interpret this spread?

Ancestors of a Generational Incarnation

All generations go through an event that alters a lifetime or the world, either for good or for ill

The World War II generation has been called the Greatest Generation. Those coming of age in the 1930s were the Depression Generation.

An interesting subset of generational incarnations is the Lost Generation. These were a group of writers who came into adulthood during and just after World War I. They included well-knowns such as Ernest Hemingway, F. Scott Fitzgerald, T. S. Eliot, and Gertrude Stein.

But those are all recent generations. What about those of our distant past incarnations? Were you living during the war between the Russian and Swedish Empires? Perhaps you were in the generation that witnessed the start of the Reformation when Martin Luther posted his list of church abuses?

Much like the events that impacted groups, these influences changed lives of entire generations. My guess is that we have all experienced at least one astonishingly world-shaking generation.

Exercise

Once again, I'm going to ask you to trust your intuition by drawing as many cards as you like, then interpreting them as best you can. See if you can find a lifetime when you experienced a generational incarnation—one that changed the world.

If you want to narrow down a century or a place, you might want to begin with yes/no questions, such as: Was my generational incarnation in the 1600s? The easiest way to interpret yes/no questions is to draw three cards. All upright are clearly yes, all reversed clearly no. If two are upright and one reversed, the answer is also yes; if two are reversed and one upright, then also no.

Here's an easy process using the yes/no three-card idea.

1. Did I experience a generation-changing life after 1700?
   Answer: No

2. Was this lifetime in the 1400s? Answer: No

3. Was this lifetime in the 1500s? Answer No

4. Was this lifetime in the 1600s? Answer Yes

5. Was the event in the Americas? No

6. Was the event in Europe? No

7. Was the event in Asia? Yes

8. Was the event in China? No

9. Was the event in Japan? Yes

If you don't want to do the yes/no approach, get a world map and use your cards and/or pendulum to pinpoint a country. In working with these generational influences, go from big to small, i.e., world to country to region to town.

If you can narrow to a century and a place, Wikipedia can become your new best friend. Look for the most impactful events of that time and place. And because we're searching for a *generation-changing past life*, the event would need to be significant.

Just doing a cursory skim through Japanese history, it appears that the 1600s were a period when Japan became more isolationist, peace prevailed, and an enjoyment of arts and culture flourished. This period began in 1603.

My questions for tarot would be based around themes such as:

- Was I a member of the artist culture?

- Was I a member of a military group?

- Was I a member of a ruling group?

Once I narrowed down to a group using my cards, that's when I would dig into events that impacted that group in that period. Make sense?

By the way, you didn't think you were investigating a generation just for kicks, did you? No, you're doing it to see if any patterns from that lifetime are still showing up in your life today.

The most profound past life experiences stay with us, good or bad. If you go around in your present life acting like a warrior—which can be a good thing—you probably want to see during which other life the warrior was born out of necessity. I look at my own attraction to Civil War observation balloons and World War 1 biplanes, and wonder in which life that longing for the sky began.

I just had an aha moment. (Please let me know that you're having them as you read this book too.) Years ago I visited a planation in Louisiana where John James Audubon had worked as a tutor. Even then I was drawn to birds. Okay, that's something else to investigate.

Note: As you can see, ideas and memories will pop up as you do this ancestral work. When that happens, create a spread, draw cards, and see if you can hear the message or the lesson of that lifetime.

JOURNAL PROMPTS

1. An issue from my _____ lifetime is

   _____ .

2. A message from an ancestor in that life is

   _____ .

3. My first step in working on issues from this lifetime is

   _____ .

Who Were You in a Past Life?

Card 1. What do I most need to know about this past life?

Card 2. What was my gender?

Card 3. What was my family like?

Card 4. What kind of work did I do?

Card 5. What was I like as a child?

Card 6. What was I like as an adult?

Card 7. What life lesson sprang from this experience?

Card 8. Why am I being shown this life?

Card 9. What strengths did I pass from that life to my present life?

Card 10. How can I best honor that life?

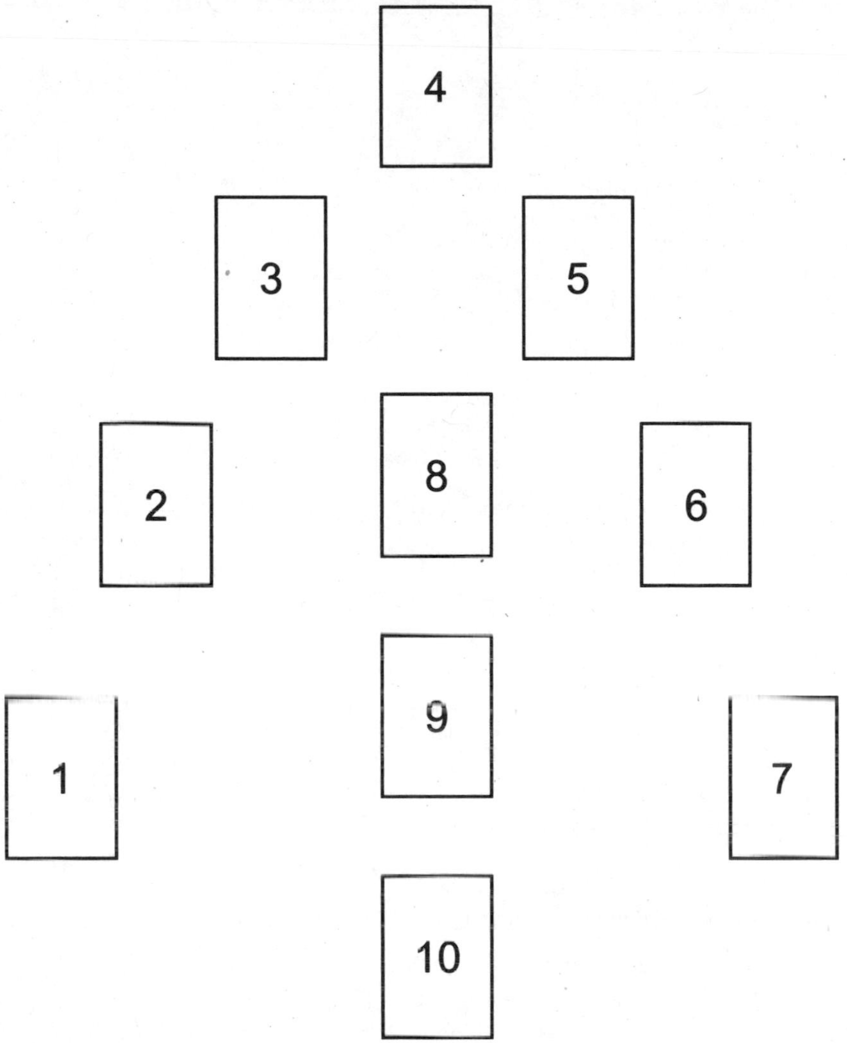
4
3
5
2
8
6
9
1
7
10

Chapter 8

Keeping an Ancestral Tarot Journal

You briefly read about journals back in chapter 3, but let's jump into tarot journaling at a deeper level.

I kept a journal for years, then became annoyed that I seemed to have the same issue year after year. So instead of working on the issues, I stopped journaling. Dumb, I know.

But then one year I started journaling a tarot card a day—mostly because I am a geeky Virgo and was curious if I would draw one suit more often than the others. What I learned after that year was that I drew more Majors than could be statistically explained. And the number of Swords far outweighed the other suits.

Once I began working with the ancestors and tarot, I started a new journal—this time tracking all my Ancestral Tarot work. I wanted a factual record of what I discovered, when I discovered it, the messages I got, and which ancestors came through. Would it surprise you to learn that on an almost daily basis the card I drew was a Cup? I feel such a close and loving affinity to the ancestors that it's almost as if there are no other cards in the deck.

If your family experiences have been fraught with discord, abuse, abandonment, or any other negatives, your cards may or may not have a prevalence of Cups—although it is possible that ancestors you never knew are there, wanting you to feel that they love you and offer protection.

If you're already doing a daily tarot practice, you can skip ahead. But if this is new for you, these are the items I recommend you include:

- your morning intent—this is a bigger deal than I ever thought it would be, as setting an intent really does color the entire day.

- which ancestor or ancestors you're working with—even if you don't know a name

- the card you drew or the spread you used

- if a spread, which cards were drawn

- your analysis of the cards

If I could draw, I'd sketch the card. As I'm hopelessly stuck with drawing stick figures, I simply do my best to sketch at least an outline of the card although it's still kindergarten-style. I also like to take the time to describe a card.

KNIGHT ⚜ PENTACLES

For example, if my card were the Knight of Pentacles, my description would be something like this: A Knight wearing a suit of armor and a plumed helmet is sitting on a black horse with red trappings. The Knight's armor is covered in red. He is holding a golden pentacle. The horse is standing still atop a green hillside and below is a plowed field. It doesn't appear as if anything has been planted yet. In the far distance are two trees and green hills. The sky behind the Knight is yellow. The Knight is wearing spurs.

If I were working with a known ancestor, I'd do my best to understand how this Knight correlated with the ancestor. I'd write about the just-plowed fields, the standing horse, and the Knight concentrating on the physical (Pentacles). I'm sure you get the drift of this type of journaling.

If possible, relate the card to a real-life event. When I looked at the Knight's big horse, I was reminded of a time I was allowed to drive (on foot) a team of four Percherons. Percherons are huge, weighing more than a Clydesdale, so you can imagine the power of holding the reins of four of them. Based on that experience, when I see the Knight of Pentacles, it tells me a lot about him because he's so at ease on that horse.

If you're wondering about the value of a daily tarot practice around ancestral work, I get it. It's a lot of work and sometimes it's pretty damned emotional. Who wants to open *that* Pandora's box? But the more you work with the ancestors using your tarot deck, the closer the connections and the deeper the healing.

DAILY INTENT

I don't want to leave your daily tarot practice without a few thoughts on *intent*. It's so easy to have an intent for the day without even realizing it. For example, if I sleep well and get up to a clear sunny sky, my unconscious intent may be that I'm going to have a great day. If I sleep poorly and wake up to gray clouds, my day may be bereft of excitement and happy anticipation. In other words, I'd go into the day feeling like crap. All this intent for what my day is going to be never even enters my conscious mind, but it is with me even so.

Once I started drawing a card for my intent for the day, things changed. I don't hop out of bed like a whirlwind, but the card does force me to consider exactly what I intend to make of the day. This morning, for example, I drew the Knight of Wands. He is confident, focused, and won't stop until he meets his goal for the day. Neither will I.

GETTING TO KNOW YOU JOURNAL SPREAD

You've already seen a lot of spreads throughout the book. But I particularly like this one when beginning to work with an ancestor I might have known in my lifetime or only known *of,* as they passed over before I was born—like

Josie. If you haven't started tarot journaling, this is a great spread to begin the practice.

For this spread you'll need to separate your deck into three piles. If you're not sure which ancestor you'll be working with, draw a card or cards that guide you to the side of the family, i.e., your mom's side or your dad's side.

Card 1. You'll begin with drawing one card from the Courts that represents you right now as you begin working with this new ancestor.

Card 2. Pull another Court to represent the ancestor as they were in life.

Card 3. Draw another Court showing their relationship with you as you begin this work.

Card 4. Select this one from the Majors to indicate the energy that will best assist your work together.

Card 5. Recombine the three stacks and draw from the whole deck for a message from this ancestor about a hard lesson they learned but are hoping to help you with so you don't have to learn it.

Here's a sample (on facing page) to help you understand what can be accomplished with this spread.

Ancestor: The grandfather I never knew and whose identity was not discovered until my mother was ninety years old.

- Me, as I begin this work (Card 1): Page of Cups (eager to make an emotional connection)

- Ancestor as they were in life (Card 2): Knight of Cups (a romantic)

- Relationship with me now (Card 3): Knight of Pentacles (slow and steady—my trust level is low)

- Energy for working together (Card 4): The Chariot (Let's get going!)

- Lesson they want to pass down (Card 5): Ten of Pentacles (learning more about his family and who he really was)

The next step, for me, would be to journal about these cards and my feelings concerning them. I'm hoping that journaling—and perhaps a few action cards—will help me understand and release my anger.

ADDING ASTROLOGY TO YOUR TAROT JOURNAL PRACTICE

As you do your daily tarot practice, you'll be meeting ancestors that you want to know from a 30,000-foot panoramic perspective. You want to get a broad picture of their life. With astrology's help, you can do this. This is a great exercise to add to your Ancestral Tarot journal.

In addition, if you do this reading for two people in the same family—particularly spouses—you'll be pulling back the curtain on what life in the relationship was really like. That's valuable information when it comes to your ancestral work.

In this exercise you'll first choose the ancestor with whom you want to work. Next, draw a circle, divided into the twelve astrological houses. (Or you can photocopy this one.)

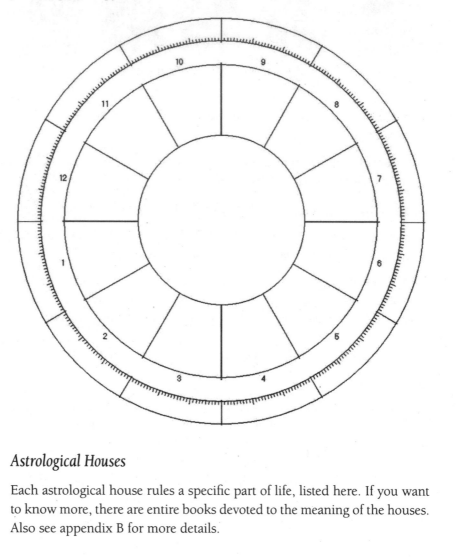

Astrological Houses

Each astrological house rules a specific part of life, listed here. If you want to know more, there are entire books devoted to the meaning of the houses. Also see appendix B for more details.

First House: Self, body

Second House: Your possessions, the things you value

Third House: Communication, siblings

Fourth House: Mom, Dad, home (This is an important one for
ancestor work.)

Fifth House: Children, creativity

Sixth House: Health, work

Seventh House: Relationships, partnerships

Eighth House: Inheritance, death

Ninth House: Higher education, long-distance travel

Tenth House: Profession, public image

Eleventh House: Friendships, community

Twelfth House: Secrets, hidden life

Digging Into the Charts

The quick and easy method of doing this spread is to draw one card per
house, but that's not going to give you the depth of information you may
want. I prefer using a method that offers more information.

Since I don't want to understand this person on a superficial level,
for this exercise you'll need to divide your deck into Minors, Majors, and
Courts. You'll then be drawing one card from each pile per house, using
a total of thirty-six cards. You'll want to use two or more decks for this as
you move forward. To make sure each house has an equal chance for all
the cards, put the drawn card back into its pile or use several decks if you
have them.

Majors will represent the theme of that person's life as it relates to the house, the Courts their personality while "wearing that house cloak," and the Minors their everyday life.

Tip: If you're a little shaky on how to interpret a tarot card within the confines of an astrological house, do this reading first for some-one—living or not—that you know well. This approach will be a lot easier once you've done the reading a couple of times with your friends or a family member. Like most tarot-based spreads, it's about taking the time to practice.

One last way to use this spread is to draw a second circle that represents you, then compare your thirty-six cards in their twelve houses with those of your ancestor. I'm pretty sure you can imagine just how eye-opening this type of reading is going to be.

Since you're using two or more decks, it's possible—and probable—that you and this ancestor are going to share some of the cards as well as some of the energy of a house. My ancestor (Grandfather H.) and I both had the King of Wands in the Twelfth House. Now here's what's freaky about that: the Twelfth House is about secrets and hidden things.

My sister had a large framed print that once belonged to this grand-father. One year, at Christmas, she took the print down to replace it with a wreath. She noticed a flash of red at the back of the print. Prying off the wooden slats, she found an 1800s sampler (sewing stuff) that was written in Hebrew. As the family isn't Jewish—although my grandfather has a Jew-ish first name—why was that sampler hidden? What was Grandpa up to? I guess I shouldn't be surprised, as he was the one who was involved in séances back in the day.

The second thing of note in my compatibility chart was the Sixth House—the House of Work. My grandfather's card was the Lovers; mine was the Hierophant. I remember a family story about Grandpa saying he only wanted two vacations a year—both six months each! His Lovers and my Hierophant are so opposite one another! I wonder what advice he would have for me about my world of work?

I'm sure you're quickly seeing what questions crop up as you do a comparative spread. It's interesting to see what message they may have for you in an area that they clearly navigated better than you do.

By the way, I did ask Gramps for a message about being less Hierophant-y with my work. He sent over the Six of Pentacles—give a little, take a little, find more balance. Based on his six-month vacation comment, it's very amusing that I drew a Six card.

Sacred Tools: Petitions

A petition is a written request with a clearly stated intention. If you Google "petitions," you will find several references to elaborate rituals using petitions in spells, candle work, and hoodoo. If this is your heritage, then you probably know what to do. For me, a petition is simple, such as

- *Dear* _____ *(name of Ancestor), my intention is that I understand why you* _____ *during your lifetime and from that understanding I will find healing.*

  Or,

- *Dear* _____ *(name of Ancestor), my intention is that I receive a message from you that helps me understand* _____.

The petition can end with Amen, Thank You, So Be It, Ah-Ho, or whatever you prefer.

There are many petition traditions such as placing the petition under a burning candle for a set period of time. Others burn the petition, then release the ashes via running water. Washing away the ashes is symbolic of releasing your hopes and wishes with a faith that they will be heard and acted upon.

While some leave the petition intact and bury it within the Earth Mother, I prefer burning it and letting the smoke carry my petition upward to Spirit. I keep dried rosemary on hand (thanks to my local climate it grows here year-round) and will often add a sprig to the burning. As Mr. Shakespeare wrote, "There's rosemary, that's for remembrance."

How does a petition differ from a prayer? A prayer can be any communication, while a petition is a request.

If you've never written a petition, begin by creating a clear intention of your desire. Then word it in your own voice. You don't have to sound religious or sermon-y, just write it as you would say it.

Chapter 9

Pairing Up

If you've ever thought it would be cool to associate the major themes of an ancestor's life with tarot's Major Arcana, you're in luck. About fifty years ago the late Angeles Arrien, writing in *The Tarot Handbook*, included a method of using a person's date of birth to calculate personality and soul numbers. Those numbers corresponded to cards in the Major Arcana. If, for example, your birth date numbers totaled four and thirteen, your numbers would correspond to the Emperor and Death.

The author and tarot authority Mary K. Greer took Arrien's work several steps further, writing first in *Tarot Constellations* and later an expanded deep dive in *Who Are You in the Tarot?* Greer's work is now considered the seminal text on what is commonly known as Birth Pairs or Birth Cards.

In brief, Birth Pairs are the two or three tarot cards that are the guiding principles of your life. Once you get into Birth Pair work, you'll want a copy of Mary's book, *Who Are You in the Tarot?* (Weiser Books, 2011). Trust me on this one.

For me, Birth Pairs show the two ends of the spectrum on which a person operates. I know that's a pretty simple way of looking at them, but it's one I find to be generally accurate. Most people easily relate to one card of the pair but find the other a challenge. For example, I am so a Hierophant but have to work harder at the Temperance end.

If you know a birth date, using Birth Pairs is one of the best ways I know to look at an ancestor's life from a thematic point of view. Was a life one of addiction (Devil/Lovers) or of adherence to a higher law (Justice/High Priestess)? Let's see.

How to Calculate Birth Pairs

There are a couple of methods used in Birth Pair calculations. I'll show you two, then tell you which one I use.

In brief, you'll be adding the number of your month, day, and year of birth. Once a total is reached, reduce it until the number is twenty-two or less. (I know that twenty-one or less is generally accepted to be "the best way" to determine Birth Pairs, but I glide a little off that flight path. More below.)

Method 1: For someone born on June 13, 1981, the calculation would be broken down into four sets of two each. Sounds harder than it is.

6 (June) + 13 (day) + 19 + 81 = 119. Next, reduce 119 to a total that's less than 22. 1 + 1 + 9 = 11. The tarot card associated with 11 is Justice. Taking it one step further, reduce any double-digit number under 22 to a single digit. In this way, 11 (1 + 1) becomes 2. This person's Birth Pair is 11/2, or Justice/High Priestess

Method 2: Pretty much the same as Method 1, except instead of adding the four-digit year in two groups of two (19 + 81), it's added to the month and day as a single number.

So 6 + 13 + 1981 = 2000. Reducing that to a number 22 or less is 2 (2 + 0 + 0 + 0). That would make the person's Birth Pair 2 (High Priestess) with an implied second number of 20 (Judgement)—the number that would reduce to a 2.

You can see from this example that you'll sometimes get a different outcome depending on the method you use. It doesn't matter which method you use, but pick one and stick to it. I use Method 2, for no other reason than it's an easy calculation.

The Oddballs: Single and Triple Digits

For some people, your calculation won't come out so neatly.

My month, day, and year of birth add up to 23 (more than 22), and this number reduces to 5. So I don't have another card to make up my pair.

In this case, the second card is implied. For me, that second card would be the Major Arcana that would reduce to 5, in this case 14, Temperance. So my Birth Pair is 14/5, Temperance/Hierophant.

But what if you're like Steve Jobs whose February 24, 1955, birth date adds up to 19? (I'm using Method 2.) The number 19 (Sun) reduces to 10 (1 + 9), which reduces to 1 (1 + 0), giving Jobs a Sun/Wheel/Magician Birth Pair (or, in this case, Triplet). A birth date totaling 19 is the only time a person will have three cards as a Birth Pair.

The Disagreed-Upon 22

While some people only work with Pairs from 1 (Magician) to 21 (World), thus excluding Card 0 (Fool), I'm not in that camp. I think if the combined birth date number is 22, then that person's Birth Pair is 22 (Fool) and 4 (Emperor).

In all of the Birth Pair work I've personally done, I've come across only one person with a 22/4 calculation. And what a tightrope their life has been. All you must do is envision one person who is like the Fool and the other who is like the Emperor. One is naive, the other confident. One is mystery, the other is mastery. A challenging life for sure.

As you do your Birth Pair calculations, whether you decide to reduce to a number equal to or less than 21 or 22 is entirely up to you. But again, pick a system and stick to it.

Birth Pair Combinations

In this system, there are thirteen Birth Pair combinations, each with its own dynamic and set of boundaries.

World/Empress—Completion, Fulfillment/Creativity, Abundance

Judgement/High Priestess—Rebirth, Awakening/Intuition, Mysteries

Sun/Wheel/Magician—Joy, Life/Cycles, Change/Creation, Manifestation

Moon/Hermit—Illusion, Delusion/Solitude, Reflection

Star/Strength—Hope, Faith/Courage, Confidence

Tower/Chariot—Upheaval, Revolution/Will, Control

Devil/Lovers—Excess and Sensuality/Choices and Unity

Temperance/Hierophant—Alchemy, Blending/Dogma, Authority

Death/Emperor—End of one cycle, beginning of another/Authority, Structure

Hanged Man/Empress—Sacrifice, New Perspectives/Creativity, Abundance

Justice/High Priestess—Fairness, Karma/Wisdom, Intuition

Wheel/Magician—Cycles, Change/Creation, Manifestation

Emperor/Fool—Authority, Structure/Innocence, Trust

Birth Pairs and the Minor Arcana

The Major Arcana (from 1, the Magician, to 10, the Wheel) each "rule" their numerical equivalent in the Minor Arcana.

Magician	The Aces		Lovers	The Sixes
High Priestess	The Twos		Chariot	The Sevens
Empress	The Threes		Strength	The Eights
Emperor	The Fours		Hermit	The Nines
Hierophant	The Fives		Wheel of Fortune	The Tens

As I stated earlier, although we weave back and forth between our two Birth Pair cards, there is probably one of the two that you're more comfortable with. The second of the pair is likely more challenging. The Minors associated with 1–10 work in a similar way. If you look at the Minor Arcana associated with your Birth Pair, there will be one or more that you actually like and find to be more of a gift than a challenge. For example, let's look at the Minor Arcana associated with Strength (8).

For you, the Eight of Wands and Eight of Pentacles may be right in your wheelhouse, while the Cups and Swords are your nemesis. For me, the Eight of Cups is a gift because it gives me permission to walk away from what appears to be good and to seek a truer path.

Because my Birth Pair is Temperance/Hierophant (14/5), my Minor Arcana are all of the Fives. There's no doubt about it, the Fives are all challenging because they're the metaphysical equivalent of a swift kick in the butt.

The gift for me is the Five of Pentacles because I know I can rely on my spiritual friendships to help me when I'm worrying about the future. My challenge is the Five of Swords. There's a constant battle going on in my brain between competing ideas. I'm not sure which to pick because I don't want to end up with an idea that's a loser. Perfectionism strikes again. This Five has troubled me for a lifetime.

Get your deck and pull out your Birth Pair and the Minor Arcana associated with it. Are there ones that you're intuitively drawn to? If so, they probably symbolize something you do well or something that, over your life, has been a blessing.

Are there any of the four Minors that make you grimace? If so, these are the cards that are challenging you *within the framework of your Birth Pair.* In other words, the "grimace" cards are the everyday events that become your growth lessons as you navigate between one Major and the other.

How to Work with Birth Pairs
and the Ancestors

Before we get started with an ancestor's Birth Pair, calculate your own Birth Pair.

Next, pick an ancestor whose birth date you know and calculate their Birth Pair. If you knew the person prior to their passing, there are a couple of things you might notice. First, the Birth Pair might seem totally out of sync with what you know of the person, or one card seems dead-on while the other appears totally off.

Here are some things to consider when working with an ancestor's Birth Pair:

Most of us wear a mask at least part of our lives or around certain groups of people. The mask could relate to work or how a person self-identifies. This means you may see someone in a very different way from their true self, only because they wear a mask to protect or hide themselves.

Here's one way to think about it, throwing a little astrology into the mix: The sign that's associated with the Chariot is Cancer the Crab. You may not see the true depth of your Chariot person because, like the Crab, he's partially inside a shell.

Here's another one. Justice is associated with Libra (the Scales). The Justice card traditionally showed Lady Justice holding a set of scales . . . weighing one thing against another. I don't know if you are acquainted with any Libras, but they will walk a million miles to avoid an argument in an effort to keep those scales in balance. While your Libra friend may always look calm and cool, the truth is that they struggle to stay in balance.

Don't dismiss an ancestor's Birth Pair just because it doesn't show the person you thought you knew.

Another thing to keep in mind is that we drift back and forth between the two Birth Pair cards throughout our lives. We can be one thing, then circumstances lead us down the second path. When I want to establish my absolute authority, I am the Hierophant. Otherwise I slide down the scale toward my more give-and-take Temperance. Too much Hierophant and I can be a self-righteous pain in the butt; too much Temperance and I'm way too wishy-washy.

Once you know your own Birth Pair and those of the ancestor you'd like to work with, compare them. It's possible how you go through life and how they went through life were not only opposite one another but in all-out conflict. Or you may share the same Birth Pair. Knowing the ancestor's Birth Pair, you will be prepared with the questions you want to ask of this ancestor and can more readily interpret the cards you draw for each question in a tarot spread.

One of my grandmothers had the Birth Pair of World/Empress. In all honesty, I can't even *begin* to see her in this way. That's because we had a less-than-perfect relationship. Set her World/Empress next to my Temperance/Hierophant and you can easily see that she actually went through life with far less rigidity than I sometimes do.

Also I never saw her as creative (Empress), but in retrospect she created all the time. My sister reminds me that Grandma never sat down that she wasn't knitting or crocheting or quilting. She was also a master gardener, and I can't remember any house she lived in that didn't have a big vegetable garden. This is the same woman who did that folk magic thing on my wrist.

It's just that Gram's brand of creativity and mine were so different that I saw her through the rigid and (frankly) persnickety lens of the Hierophant.

Did I mention that the astrological correspondence to the Hierophant is Taurus. Just try and move that bull off an opinion once it's set.

What Happens if You Don't Have a Birth Date?

There are multiple records that include birth dates (see sidebar), but one that is often overlooked is a tombstone. The only time you may run into difficulty is when you find a tombstone that has an inscription like this: Died March 5, 1885, aged 71 yrs, 8 mos, 3 days. Face-palm. How do you calculate backward to find out the birth date?

Someone way smarter than I wrote a computer utility that does the math for you. If you do run into this problem, pop over here to the FamilySearch Date Calculator (*www.familysearch.org*), put in the date you know (March 5, 1885) along with the years, months, and days of life and you'll see that this person was born on July 2, 1813. Pretty cool.

Otherwise, you'll have to rely on family info or officialdom like a marriage license or birth certificate.

Where to find birth dates?

- Birth certificates
- Marriage licenses
- Death certificates
- Land records
- Probate files
- Federal census
- State census
- Church records
- Baptismal records

- Court documents

- Home records

- Military enlistments

- Newspaper obituaries

- Published sources

- Tax records

- Draft registrations

DEATH PAIRS

If Birth Pairs show the path we walk in this life, do Death Pairs signify the path taken into the afterlife? Are they a neat wrap-up of a lifetime? This is a topic that's been on my mind for a very long time. While I can't prove Death Pairs any more than I can prove that praying over a dead snake brings rain, I have gathered enough anecdotal evidence to believe Death Pairs are a valid approach to ancestral work.

Birth Pairs accompany us throughout life, but as we approach the end of this incarnation, do we release our Birth Pairs much like we'd shed our skin, then begin to take on the Death Pairs that will guide us home?

Death Pairs are calculated exactly as Birth Pairs, except the date used is the date of death.

If someone came into this life with the Birth Pair of Tower/Chariot and left with the same two cards, doesn't that tell you something about the person, their life, aspirations, and (perhaps) even fatalistic feelings about life and death?

I want to know that the people I loved left this incarnation with a sense of completion or at least peace. If I had difficulties with someone during this lifetime, it's my hope that understanding both their Birth and Death Pairs will leave me with more a sense of serenity than one of resentment, judgment, or animosity.

If you know the Birth and Death Pairs of an ancestor who lived and died before you were born, you now have one more tool to communicate with them, gain knowledge about their lives, and hopefully find a strength in *their life* that filters down to your own.

Again, note the pairs in your journal for whichever ancestor you want to work with. Later, in chapter 10, you'll add these cards to their Whole Self Mandala.

Sample Death Pairs

Let's look at a few well-known people who have passed over and see what their Death Pairs might tell us.

Note: My calculations are based on Method 2 in Birth Pairs.

Steve Jobs was the creative mind and life force energy behind Apple, Inc. I think we can all agree that his lifework changed the world.

Birth Pair: Jobs was born on February 24, 1955, giving him a Birth Pair of 19/10/1 (the Sun, the Wheel, the Magician). In their broadest terms, the Sun represents joy, the Wheel is change (or fate), and the Magician is creation or manifestation.

Death Pair: Steve passed on October 5, 2011, giving him a Death Pair of 10/1 (the Wheel and the Magician). In a literal as well as metaphorical sense, the Sun had set on his life—but the magic did not.

Here's another person to consider: John F. Kennedy, the thirty-fifth president of the United States and the first U.S. president born in the twentieth century.

Birth Pair: Kennedy was born on May 29, 1917, giving him a Birth Pair of 16/7 (Tower/Chariot). Keywords are upheaval or destruction and will or control. Was he born to shake up the norm and bring it to his will?

Death Pair: Kennedy died on November 22, 1963, with a Death Pair of a single 7 with 16 implied. Again, this is Tower/Chariot. There are numerous references to Kennedy's illness-filled childhood and near death in World War II. It's almost as if the Tower/Chariot duo were pursuing him throughout life.

While these two cases tend toward the extreme, I think they give us clues about the paths those passing take as they cross over.

I encourage you to use Wikipedia to look up well-known figures and calculate both birth and death dates, then experiment with how well their Birth and Death Pairs fit into your understanding of a person.

A word of caution: Prior to 1752, the Julian calendar was used, but in that year Britain and her colonies changed to the Gregorian calendar. So if you want to do a Birth Pair for George Washington, for example, just be aware that he was born on February 11, 1731 (Julian calendar) but when the Gregorian calendar was adopted, Washington's birth date became February 22, 1732. Confusing, huh?

I prefer using whichever calendar was in effect at the time of someone's birth. That means Washington would have a Birth Pair of 7 with an implied 16 (another person born to revolution!), under his original Julian calendar date. His Death Pair would then be calculated under the Gregorian system as that was in effect at the time of his death on December 14, 1799. Guess what? That pair is also Tower/Chariot.

I decided to calculate one more U.S. president, George H. W. Bush (41st). Born on June 12, 1924, his Birth Pair is 16/7 (Tower/Chariot). Bush passed away on November 30, 2018, with a Death Pair of 16/7 (Tower/ Chariot).

Hmm, it seems I'm seeing a recurring pattern here!

But seriously, not all world leaders walk the Tower/Chariot Death Pair. Margaret Thatcher, the first female prime minister of the United Kingdom, has a Birth Pair of 4 (Emperor) with an implied 13 (Death) and a Death Pair of 9 (Hermit) with an implied 18 (Moon). One of the secondary causes of her death was dementia—a very Hermit and Moon–like pair.

One other prime minister, however, was born a 16/7—Winston Churchill—but when he passed, his Death Pair was 19/10/1 (Sun, Wheel, Magician). Does his mean he, too, was born to revolution and left as a great shining sun over the British Empire?

Here are a few more well-known personalities to consider—but remember, the face we see of a public figure may be far removed from the face without the public persona mask on, so take these with a grain of salt:

Alexander Hamilton—Temperance/Hierophant

Marilyn Monroe—Hanged Man/Empress or World/Empress, depending on how you calculate

Anthony Bourdain—Tower/Chariot

Luke Perry—Wheel/Magician

Danny Aiello—Moon/Hermit

Jimi Hendrix—Star/Strength

Amy Winehouse—Tower/Chariot

Mark Twain—Moon/Hermit

Kate Spade—Death/Emperor

Stephen Hawking—Wheel/Magician

You know I could go on and on, but for now, Google several other people you have an interest in, and calculate their Death Pairs. What do you think? Viable information or iffy?

The problem, of course, is an obvious one. Unless you knew someone well enough to have insight into the period when they left this incarnation, the numbers may not make sense to you. My advice is to use the numbers for an ancestor you knew, and then once you have confidence in the process, you can apply this method for other ancestors with whom you wish to work.

How to Use Death Pairs

By now, I'm hoping you've calculated Death Pairs for several ancestors. Here's how to use them.

Go back to the ancestor you worked with in Birth Pairs, laying out your initial draw for them. If you don't remember, or didn't write it down, go ahead and pull out their Birth Pair cards and then their Death Pair cards.

Questions to ask:

- Do you see any patterns?

- Is there something about the person that makes you want to work with them even further?

- Are there similarities or dissimilarities between their Death Pair and (perhaps) the Birth or Death Pairs of a spouse?

- Does knowing their Death Pair give you a sense of closure and peace or does it generate more questions?

In my own family, my mom passed away with a Death Pair of 11/2, Justice/High Priestess. Because I spent an enormous amount of time with her in the two years preceding her passing, I know without a doubt that her final voyage was accepted, and in fact embraced. Her life balance sheet was even. She left with all debts paid. Her knowingness about the hereafter was confirmed to her by the presence of her own long-deceased mother who stood by her toward the end.

My dad, on the other hand, had a Birth Pair of 17/8 (Star/Strength) and passed with a Death Pair of 16/7, again Tower/Chariot. Dad died at age forty-four of a sudden and massive heart attack. He left this incarnation with upheaval and an instant passing. I think the Chariot took him so swiftly he knew nothing until reaching the other side.

What if You Don't Know a Death Date?

People who trace their family history are cemetery junkies. I discovered a few years ago there's a word for people who are cemetery-obsessed, and the word is *taphophile*. Kind of creepy sounding, I think. But there it is . . . we haunt cemeteries hoping to track down places where family were buried. If you can find a tombstone, you'll generally have a date of death, but unless the inscription is written in English, you'll need a service like Google Translate. However, even Google can't translate words using a different alphabet system such Greek or Hebrew. For that, you'll need a translator or an online forum of native speakers. For example, I've used *JewishGen.org* for help in translating Hebrew.

There are a couple of great websites—both free—where you can search for a grave. Believe it or not, thousands of cemeteries have been well-documented over the year. The sites are *FindaGrave.com* and *BillionGraves.com*. Sometimes you'll see only a death year, not the entire date. At either site you can request that a volunteer take a tombstone photo for you—that way you can see the dates unless the stone is too deteriorated to read.

If the deceased was buried in an American National Cemetery, you're in luck as there's a Nationwide Gravesite Locator—also free—that lists information for anyone buried in one at https://gravelocator.cem.va.gov/.

Cemetery Symbolism

If your ancestors were buried 100 years ago or so, you can get to know something important about their life from their tombstone. This is especially true if they passed over up until the mid-twentieth century.

Back in the day, a tombstone wasn't just used to denote where a person was buried. The designs on the stone were specific to that individual and their beliefs. Tombstone symbols—just like the ones on tarot cards—are clues about the person or the people they left behind. You can Google "cemetery symbols" and find the meanings of dozens, but among the most common are:

- Crosses—There are lots of crosses, so do a little research. For example, a Celtic Cross is going to have a different meaning than a Christian cross.

- Lambs—Lambs are mostly seen sitting atop a child's grave. They symbolize innocence.

- Tree stump—This is when the tombstone is in the actual shape of a tree stump. It symbolizes a life cut short.

- Upward-pointing finger—My own great-grandfather has this one on his tombstone. It's all about going to heaven.

- Open book—This can symbolize either the Bible or the Book of Life.

- Weeping willow—This one is more about the person left behind and their sadness.

- Downward-pointing finger—God is reaching down for the person.

Symbols vary by country and culture as well. For example, thanks to Napoleon's journey to Egypt, you'll find Egyptian symbolism on many Parisian graves. If you get a tombstone photo, don't look only for dates; check out the symbols too.

One More to Consider—Event Pairs

What if a person experienced an event so tragic or so joyful that it skewed their Birth Pair down *not a new path*, but an *expanded path*? Let me explain.

In numerology, the name you are given at birth is used to compute your personality, how others see you, and why you do the things you do. If you get married or change your name, you don't lose the numbers from your birth name; instead you take on the additional numbers of your new name.

Although I believe that a person's Birth Pair shows us the parameters within which a life is lived, sometimes circumstances can throw a monkey wrench into our carefully plotted calculations and our oh-so-orderly plans of incarnation. While an event won't change your Birth Pair, it can add another layer to the parameters you experience.

Let's say that someone was born under the Star/Strength energy of hope and courage. But what if, at a critical life juncture, they experienced the horrors of war, the ravages of disease, or some other horrific event? I believe they still operate between Star/Strength, but I also believe that they reach a point where we need to look at yet another factor: The "birth" date of the life-altering event.

Let me give you an example. What if a person was born with a Birth Pair of Moon/Hermit but a tragic event occurred on a Wheel/Magician day? Is it possible that this person might experience that tragedy as something they were profoundly lucky to escape, thus changing their worldview? Think about it.

If an Event Pair is something that altered your ancestor's life—as far as you can tell—be sure to note it in your journal so it can be added to the Whole Self Mandala.

I'm going to take this concept a step further—to how a Birth Pair can be impacted by an Event Pair. If you look at the Birth Pair for the United States, based on July 4, 1776, you'll get 5 (Hierophant) with an implied 14

(Temperance). By the way, numerologically, five is the number for change—and what a big change that was.

Next, add in two significant events, one in the twentieth century, the other in the twenty-first century: the assassination of John F. Kennedy (November 22, 1963) and the terrorist attack of September 11, 2001. Both of those dates had a huge impact on the country: Kennedy's death a Tower/Chariot (16/7) and 9/11 a Temperance/Hierophant (14/5).

Did those events add a life layer to anyone who lived through them? The Kennedy assassination certainly turned the world upside down. And what did 9/11 do? It made the United States and a good portion of the world much more cautious, almost as if everyone retreated into the Hierophant space, then, like Temperance, tried to find ways to live with a new reality.

Let's look at one more public person: Jacqueline Kennedy Onassis. Born a 20/2 (Judgment/High Priestess), the date of JFK's assassination was a 16/7 (Tower/Chariot). Did she take on part of that 16/7 energy? That's an unknown and probably always will be, but we absolutely saw a drastic lifestyle change following that event, didn't we? Interestingly, her Death Pair was 11/2—she exchanged Judgement for Justice, but kept the High Priestess.

This is where I encourage you to work out Birth Pairs, Death Pairs, and Event Pairs (if applicable) and judge for yourself how accurate these ideas are.

JOURNAL PROMPTS

1. What was your own Birth Pair? What did you learn about yourself using Birth Pairs?

2. What ancestor did you calculate a Birth Pair for and what did you learn about them using the cards?

3. If you calculated a Death Pair, which ancestor was it for and what did it add to your understanding about how this ancestor felt at the end of life?

Chapter 10

Whole Self Mandala

I n tarot you can't use the Major Arcana without running into the concept of archetypes. But how do you translate archetypal energy into easily understandable language when it comes to describing an ancestral lifetime? Drawing the Judgement card (20) is all about walking into, or waking up to, a new life, but what exactly does that mean for your Ancestral Tarot work when it comes to Granny Joan?

And what if Granny Joan, the culprit who started a whole icky family pattern, was a King of Swords with a Six of Pentacles clarifier, living in a life of renewal (20)? How can you put these three cards together and at a deep level understand her as well as her actions? I do it using a Whole Self Mandala.

If you've ever been into astrology, you'll have heard something like "Her Mars is in Cancer in the tenth house." To an astrologer that statement is loaded with information because they know what Cancer means, they know what Mars means, and they know the meaning of the tenth house. All they must do is put them together in an understandable way.

Using the Whole Self Mandala, you can do the same thing with an ancestor and tarot.

In this chapter, I'm going to walk you step-by-step toward creating an ancestor's Whole Self Mandala.

STEP 1. WHICH ANCESTOR SHOULD YOU WORK WITH?

As this exercise is going to reveal the whole person as opposed to the bits you've been working with, select whom you want to create the mandala for. Choose a person that you have already worked with earlier in the book, one you know the birth date for. If you know their death date, even better, but that's optional. Your person may be the one you had the most affection for, the one who made your life miserable, or one that you knew of but didn't meet before they passed over.

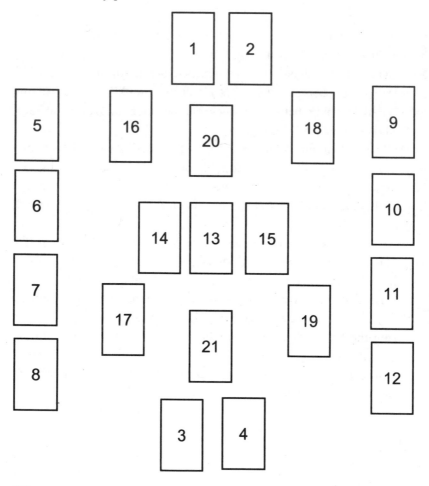

Step 2. Begin Building the Mandala

Cards 1 and 2. If you know the birth date, these are the two cards that make up the Birth Pair. Go back to chapter 9 if you've forgotten how to calculate the cards. You may have three cards here if your person was a Sun/Wheel/Magician. If you do have this triplet, just consider that the third card is 2a.

Cards 3 and 4. These are the Death Pair which you also learned about in chapter 9. If you don't know a death date, leave these two spaces blank for now.

Cards 5, 6, 7, 8. The Minor Arcana associated with the Birth Pair. For example if the Birth Pair is World/Empress, all of the Minor Arcana Threes will be here. If your person is a Sun/Wheel/Magician, you will have all the Minor Arcana Ones here as well as all of the Minor Arcana Tens. If you don't know the Birth Pair, draw four Minor Arcana cards at random.

Cards 9, 10, 11, 12. The Minor Arcana associated with the Death Pair (if known). Again, if you don't know the Death Pair, draw four Minor Arcana cards at random with the intent of learning something about the person that will help in your life today.

Because Cards 1–12 are assigned via Birth and Death Pairs, use a second deck to lay out the remaining cards 13–21. If you use the same deck, it will greatly reduce the possibilities of the draw.

Card 13. How did this ancestor view their life? (It's optional, but you may want to draw this card from the Major Arcana only.)

Card 14. What did this ancestor wish they could go back and change?

Card 15. What is this ancestor most proud of?

Card 16. How will working more deeply with this ancestor impact my life?

Card 17. What is one piece of advice this ancestor wants to give me?

Card 18. What kind of person does the ancestor think they were? (Draw from the Courts.)

Card 19. What kind of person was the ancestor really? (Draw from the Courts.)

Card 20 and 21. What do I still need to learn about this ancestor?

If you know the death date of this ancestor, be sure to add the Death Pair to the mandala. If you do not know the death date of this ancestor, you can either leave spaces 3 and 4 open, or add in two more questions that you feel are important for you in working with this ancestor. If you are fortunate enough to know Event Pairs for this person, add those to the mandala as well. Where you place them in the design is up to you.

Optional: Draw one card and place it horizontally across the bottom of the mandala for each decade of the ancestor's life. I found this addition fascinating as the truly joyous cards for my person were for the decade that he married as well as the decade in which he had children.

For positions 13–21, once I drew a card, I replaced it in the deck. That's why, in my sample, you'll see the same card more than once. You can also use multiple decks if you prefer.

STEP 3. ANALYZE WHAT YOU'VE LEARNED

If you have built a mandala in order to continue healing with an ancestor you knew, where do you start in understand the whole?

First, look at the Birth and Death Pairs—if available—and the Minor Arcana that belong to both. In my draw, the Birth Pair was Death/Emperor, which gave the ancestor all the Fours.

For your ancestor, what do the Birth Pair and their Minors tell you?

If your Death Pair showed up as World/Empress, with all the Threes of the Minor Arcana, what might this indicate about the ancestor's waning time in this incarnation?

Isn't this a good time to sketch the layout in your journal, note your cards, and put down your first impressions?

Next, begin by searching for patterns beginning with Card 13.

- How many cards of each suit were drawn?

- How many Major Arcana cards are showing?

- How many cards with the same number are there?

Sample Person

In the sample person (shown on page 162), Cards 13–21, you'll see there are seven Cups and two Major Arcana. There were no Swords, no Pentacles, no Wands. The Queen of Cups appeared twice as did the Three of Cups

Card 13, how the ancestor saw their life was the Star. Next, look at the two cards in the 14 and 15 positions: What they wish they could go back and change (Six of Cups) and what they're most proud of (Three of Cups).

Now, go to Cards 16 and 17: How working with this ancestor impacts your life and the piece of advice from the ancestor. The sample shows the Knight of Cups and Temperance.

Card 18 and 19 show the difference between who the ancestor thinks they were and who they really were. Our draw showed the King of Cups and Queen of Cups.

The last pair, Cards 20 and 21, are the things that you still need to learn about the ancestor. My draw was the Queen of Cups and the Three of Cups.

Although it is not shown in this illustration, I did draw cards for the decades of his life, getting five Major Arcana and the King of Cups.

If this were your ancestor, what conclusions or impressions would you have about them at this point?

As you work with this spread more, choosing different ancestors, a tremendous amount of information is going to be revealed. The spread is also a flex spread—as you have more questions or want more clarification, you are free to add more positions, more cards, and more clarifiers.

Who Was This Person?

If I had to come up with an interpretation based on a quick glance at this mandala, the first thing that I'd say is that this person was family-oriented, loved having a good time, and probably was a person you'd love sitting next to at a party.

What a life this must have been when the answer to "what do you wish you could go back and change?" was the Six of Cups and the "what are you most proud of?" was the Three of Cups. To reach out from beyond and say that they wished they could have spent more time with the kids when they were young—that's the message I heard—but to also say that they were proud of the fact that they celebrated wins, both big and small, now that's something.

How interesting it is that the advice for me was Temperance and the impact of working with them is going to be the Knight of Cups.

How would you interpret these cards?

WHAT DID YOU LEARN FROM YOUR MANDALA?

I know this spread takes some time and definitely some thought. But now that you've laid out up to twenty-one cards—or more if you pulled a card for the decades—what do you think? Do you feel that the cards you drew gave you a deeper understanding of this person? Did it answer some questions or did it generate even more?

Ancestral Tarot is an ongoing practice. If the healing you want didn't come out of the cards you just drew, then ask for clarification—or ask a different question or ask it of a different ancestor. If you had an issue with your now-deceased mother and you can't get an answer that helps with your healing, ask *her* mother or *her* father or her mother's mother to help. Someone in the family holds the key.

I believe that no matter how well you do Ancestral Tarot work, there are some family issues that may never be revealed, never talked about, or never confronted. But through your use of tarot and the spreads throughout the book, it's my hope that you find exactly what you need by touching base with exactly the right ancestor.

That's the great thing about working with the ancestors. Don't like one generation? Then go back further in time to another.

JOURNAL PROMPTS

1. I choose _____ for a Whole Self Mandala because

_____ .

2. The thing that surprised me the most about _____ was

_____ .

3. The ways I differ from _____ are

_____

_____

The ways we are alike are

_____

_____ .

Chapter 11

Ancestral Rituals

Honoring ancestors is probably as old a practice as humankind. The ancestors gave us life and have an interest in our happiness and success. In return, they want to be remembered. After all, had they not existed, neither would you.

Not so many years ago I scrambled down a canyon wall in Northern Arizona and hiked along a narrow trail until reaching a flat rock face. On it was chipped the story of a people who lived there hundreds of years earlier. Men and bobcats, spirals and deer—a memoir in stone.

As I placed my palm flat against the rock, I knew I was touching a life that wanted to be remembered. Were they my Ancestors of Time? I have no idea, but I do know that they, like all the ancestors, reach out for remembrance. In this chapter, I'll show you how to do that.

SACRED SPACE

If you don't already have a sacred space in which to do this work, it's time to set one up.

Regardless of where you do ancestral work—or tarot readings for that matter—you need to establish an energy that is sacred and dedicated to your purpose. Sacred space makes it easier to ground yourself in your work. It also lets the ancestors know that you're approaching them in a respectful manner.

Although I can read tarot in a coffeehouse, without first establishing a bubble of sacred energy around me, the reading has more of a two-dimensional rather than a three-dimensional feel. It's like rattling off the meaning of the cards without gathering in their energy as a whole, along with the energy of the querent's question.

Ancestral work is the same. As I've written elsewhere, popping out a few cards and calling it done will be a disservice to you and your healing, as well as to the ancestors.

So what, exactly, is sacred space? Loosely, it's a space that has been set aside for a spiritual practice. A church or temple falls within the definition of sacred space. Within a sacred space, you can focus and dedicate your energy to ritual, healing, or divinatory work, just to name a few reasons to set aside this area. This isn't a physical space where you toss your jacket after coming in from work or set up a game board. Sacred space has a singular purpose: making the ordinary extraordinary.

Does sacred space need to be inside? Nope. Daily, I walk around my urban neighborhood. My focus (dedication) during that walk is to drink in the abundant and generous energies of the flowers, trees, and animals that cross my path. This very morning, the bird-of-paradise told me how much it loves being admired. A cheeky squirrel winked at me, peeking out from its hiding place on the far side of a palm tree.

As I walk, my own energetic space becomes sacred as it's set aside (dedicated) for part of my spiritual practice.

Sacred space is a personal concept. If you're fortunate enough to live near wild nature, you might consider sacred space the entire forest or a nearby river. For people like me who live in a multimillion-person city, there isn't a lot of *obvious* sacred space, but it is there. That's because you've created it.

The most commonly found sacred space is the place you live, whether it's a huge house or a tiny studio apartment. My place has a weird alcove with a built-in desk, located between where I work and the bathroom. I never knew what to do with it, so it became a collection point for tarot decks, spare glasses, a bowl of crystals, a chair with a jacket draped over it, a pine cone, a 1940s photo of my mom, a rune, dried pepper tree berries . . . in other words stuff that I didn't know what to do with.

Because I wanted a dedicated space for ancestral work, I decided to use my tarot deck and pendulum to find out if this alcove was the best place energetically for my work. If you have a pendulum, grab it and do this exercise along with me. If you don't have a pendulum, make one by tying a piece of string around a metal washer or nail—anything with enough weight to make it usable as a pendulum. Ask the pendulum to show you how it swings when the answer is yes, when the answer is no, and when the answer is maybe.

If your pendulum doesn't want to move at all, start it swinging by giving it a push. It will eventually settle into its own pattern of movement.

Finding Your Own Sacred Space

Next, get a blank piece of paper and draw a rough map of the rooms in your home where you think you'd like to do your spiritual work. Mine was really easy to do as I'm a minimalist at heart and live in a tiny studio. If you live in a multistory house, you have far more sketching to do than my supereasy one.

Once the rooms are sketched out—don't worry about correct dimensions—label the placement of things in the room, like your bed, bookcase, or kitchen table. Next, pull a tarot card for each room. Once you've identified the best *room* for your sacred space based on the cards, draw cards for each item within the space to see if there's a place within the room with the energy you're seeking. Here's an example of what I pulled:

- Orange Chair—Ten of Pentacles

- Bed—High Priestess

- Bookcase—Page of Swords (I had to laugh at this one—what better place for a Page of Swords than a bookcase!)

- Desk—Five of Pentacles

- Bathroom—King of Wands

- Kitchen—Knight of Pentacles

- Weird Alcove—Queen of Wands

Since I had more than one space that looked pretty good to me, I got out my pendulum and held it over each of the places I was considering. I got zero movement at everything except the orange chair and the alcove. The pendulum moved in a small, tight circle over the chair part of my map, but when it came to the alcove, it reacted so strongly it almost flew out of my hand.

You know what that meant—I had to clean up the mess I had created in the alcove to use it as sacred space.

What Does Your Space Need?

As you determine which area of your inside space you want to dedicate to your ancestral work, here are a few things to keep in mind: First, what do you need to do to make the space comfortable? Mundane, I know, but realistic. Second, how do you clear away the junk heap energy that you might have created there—like I did? Third, how do you invite the ancestors or your Spirit Guides into your space? For these three questions, I drew three tarot cards.

1. How do I make the space more comfortable? The Sun. Because the alcove is located between two living spaces, it's on the dark side, so kinda funny that the Sun made an appearance here. Better lighting and calling in the Sun energy are in order.

2. How do I clear away the junk heap energy I had created? The Six of Pentacles. Get rid of the clutter. Use your "energy feelers" to decide what to keep in that space and what to either toss or give away.

3. Lastly, how do I invite the ancestors or Spirit Guides into the space? I am perpetually surprised/not surprised at the fairylike humor of tarot. Invite the ancestors in by holding out an energy lantern. It's almost like the light in a dark window—let the light of your intent show them that they're welcome and illuminate the way.

It's fine to use your Oracle or affirmation cards as clarifiers if one of your tarot draws doesn't make any sense to you.

If you're unsure of what kind of energy you want to create for the ancestors in your sacred space, draw a card. Let's see what it says.

Well that was an interesting draw! The first thing that crossed my mind was to be outside doing this work, as nature is the most sacred space I know. The second thought—and this one cracked me up—was to go to a vineyard or buy a Groupon for wine tasting. Hey! Doing sacred work doesn't mean I can't appreciate their humor.

Space Clearing

While my tarot card gave me the basics of clearing my energetic space for ancestral work, there are other methods you can use in conjunction with your cards. If you're a crystal worker, you will know which crystals to employ for space clearing. You'll also know how best to position the stones. For me, the pattern in which I place a stone is just as important as the pattern I use to create a tarot spread. A circle will have a different energy from a spiral or a triangle.

If you want to clear space by both drawing cards and using crystals, try using the Major Arcana only. That's because there are several tarot-crystal correspondence charts online that you can easily find with Google. Later, you'll find my own Majors-crystal correlation chart under "Tarot and Crystal Grids." This isn't to say that mine is *the* one to use—it's just the one I like. Try what works for you, and over time you'll begin to create your own tarot-crystal system.

You can also use a Major Arcana card to help you decide which crystal and which shape of crystal placement to use in space clearing. For instance, if I drew the Hanged Man, I'd place my crystals in a T-shape, using stones that draw in the colors of the Hanged Man's clothes—traditionally red and blue. I would also select a stone with the same color as the golden aura around the man's head.

But what if your card is the Devil? That card, traditionally, is primarily black. For this case, I'd pick a black tourmaline, not only for its color but also for its protective properties. And the placement of stones? What's on top of the Devil's head? Yep, a pentacle.

Space clearing isn't at all limited to crystals or tarot. You may have a method you already use, like calling in certain deities or asking your guides to help clear the space. Sometimes I use votive candles of various colors, moving them into different positions like on a tarot spread until I find the design that feels right. And "feels right" means when I look at the positions and colors, the energy has a sense of balance.

If in doubt, ask the ancestors.

CREATING AN ANCESTRAL ALTAR

My guess is you may already have an altar in your home. But do you have one specifically for the ancestors? If not, read on to learn what you may want to include and how to begin building it.

First, decide whom the altar is for. Is it for a specific person, your entire maternal or paternal family lines, or all of your ancestors? An altar can be temporary or permanent. For example, if someone you admired recently passed away, you may want to create a temporary altar, giving thanks for their life and their inspiration.

If the altar is for a specific person, it may be permanent. My permanent altar is for my mother.

If you live in a large house, you may be able to dedicate a room or part of a room to one or more altars. If where you live is tiny, your altar will organically reflect the size required. Sample indoor altar placements can include a shelf, closet, desk, or even a desk drawer—although I personally don't like the idea of putting an altar inside a drawer. Again, that's just me.

If you want to follow tradition, your altar will include something representing all the elements: Earth, Wind, Fire, Water. You'll also include an altar cloth, a candle, and a photo or something representative of the person the altar is for.

As a lifelong cat whisperer, I'm supercautious about candles and prefer ones that live in tall jars. The smell of a singed cat tail is not appealing. If your home is cat-free, then any kind of candle works, if you keep an eye on it and remain aware of fire safety.

The Elements

Air. We mostly think about feathers as representing air, but you can also use images of the clouds or even a Lenormand card called the Clouds.

Earth. A piece of bark, a twig, a coin, a flower—anything that you'd find in the suit of Pentacles will do. This could also include a piece of jewelry or a crystal.

Fire. A candle works, of course, or photos of fire, flames, or a fireplace. I don't like using photos of an out-of-control forest fire or wildfire as I don't want to draw in that kind of destructive energy.

Water. The easiest way to represent water on your altar is to place a glass of water there. If you want to leave it as part of a permanent altar, change it out at least weekly.

Your altar might also include a photo of a raven, which, in folklore, carries prayers to heaven.

Outdoor Altars

Are you fortunate enough to have an outdoor space for an altar? Lucky you. One of my very favorite ways of creating an outdoor altar is to plant a memory garden. These are small—they can even be done in a large pot—or large flower beds planted with something that's reminiscent of your loved one. In all cases, I would also include rosemary for remembrance.

On a trip to the Midwest, I was able to find an old burying ground where my great-grandparents were buried. It was in a stand of timber, with weeds up to my waist. Several tombstones were turned over either by falling branches or grazing cattle. It was a miracle that the tombstones were spotted at all.

Near the ones for my family I discovered wild lilies. I asked permission of the flowers, then dug one up to take home and repot in honor of my family buried there. I've never gone back to that old burying ground, but the wild lily thrived for years near my home.

Other people I know have honored their ancestors by planting favorite flowers, taking a cutting from a tree or plant where they grew up, or growing something they associate with an ancestor. One of my favorites is the woman who planted a coreopsis, also known as moonlight, in remembrance of her grandfather who told her stories about climbing a ladder to reach the moon.

Traveling Altars

I love creating small portable altars. If you live in a place with very little space, a portable altar is a perfect choice. And when I say "small," I mean this altar is really tiny. In fact, it's built inside a tin—you know, the ones that are used for mints or breath fresheners.

How you decorate the altar is a personal decision, but I like covering mine with a picture of my ancestor or one of the homes the ancestor lived in. If I don't have a photo of either, I'll look at one of the copyright-free image sites like *Pixabay.com* and find a photo that seems to fit. Don't forget to cover the insides of the tin as well.

What could you put inside? You'll have room for a birthday-sized candle and a small gemstone. Yours may have a sprig of lavender, sage, or an herb that's meaningful for you. If you have one of those tiny tarot decks, you can also add the card that represents this ancestor. Other suggestions include

- salt
- feather
- symbol of a deity
- matches
- incense sticks
- religious symbol
- crystal chip

Choosing Stones for the Altar

Whether you build an indoor or outdoor altar, you'll probably want to use some type of crystal. The stones you choose will correlate to the tarot cards you pulled for the ancestor you want to work with. You will see my own tarot-crystal correlation later in this chapter, but as you work with stones and the ancestors, you'll be building your own reference library.

If you're uncertain of why you're building the altar or the ancestor you want an altar for, consider laying out a crystal grid of clear quartz, asking for clarity of purpose and focus. If you know that the altar is about giving and receiving ancestral love, then what better than a rose quartz. If asking the ancestors for protection, black tourmaline is a great choice. If you don't want a stone on your altar or don't have room for one, you can put it outside or just inside your door, or even under your altar.

For those lucky enough to have an outdoor space to build an altar, my suggestion would be to pull a Major Arcana, pick the stones you feel correspond with that card, then perhaps build the altar at the base of a tree, around large rocks, a water feature, or even in a large half-barrel where you've planted flowers that remind you of the ancestors. This becomes a mini-memory garden.

CEMETERIES AND THE ANCESTORS

If taking flowers to a cemetery is one of the ways you honor ancestors, then this section is for you.

Cemeteries are filled with so many energies. There is one large cemetery near my home where I photograph tombstones for people who don't live close by. This particular cemetery has special sections for Asian, Hispanic, and Jewish burials.

In the Asian section, you'll often see cans of Coke, incense, or food left to honor the departed. The Hispanic graves are brightly decorated with paper or plastic flowers, along with photos of the deceased. Jewish tombstones almost always have the name of the deceased's father written in

Hebrew at the top of the stone. And, instead of leaving flowers, small stones are placed atop the marker.

As cremation is far more common now than in our grandparents' time, there may or may not be a tombstone to commemorate the person. If the ashes were scattered, then—for me—the sacred place to honor that ancestor can either be where they were born or where their remains were scattered. If their remains were placed in a gravesite or a columbarium (wall of cremations), then that's where I'd go.

In the Western tradition, leaving flowers on a grave is a common practice. But what if you live a zillion miles away from the cemetery where your ancestors are buried? If you know where the cemetery is located, you can place virtual flowers or create a virtual memorial to the ancestor using the free website *FindAGrave.com*. Once you pinpoint the spot, just click the Leave a Flower button and you'll have several choices, including favorites like forget-me-nots, pansies, and roses. You can also leave a note with your name or you can remain anonymous.

There's a strange, but true fact you should keep in mind if you know the general site but not the specific spot of an ancestor's grave: If you're driving around a cemetery not sure of where your ancestor is buried, it's highly likely that you'll end up parking the car just a few feet from the grave. It's weird, but true. I told you they want to be remembered

How Does Your Culture Honor Ancestors?

Honoring the ancestors is far from a modern tradition. If your family always visits a cemetery on Memorial Day, then that's how you might approach honoring an ancestor. But what if your culture has different traditions? Or what if you don't know any traditions? Draw a card and ask the ancestors.

We all know the story of King Tut and how Egyptian tombs were loaded with grave goods so that the deceased would have all they need on their journey to the afterlife.

We also know that some Native American tribes sang songs and said prayers, while others blackened their faces. Still others avoid the deceased for fear of attracting the spirit of what was bad about the person.

In Mexico, *Días de los Muertos* (Days of the Dead) is celebrated during the first two days of November. This is a time when families commemorate the lives of their loved ones who have crossed over. Elaborate altars are constructed—some at the gravesite, some in the home, and others in public places. I live near the Mexican border, so my city is filled with symbols associated with *Días de los Muertos*: Marigolds are used to attract the soul of the dead back to the world of the living. Graves are cleaned and decorated, and *ofrendas* (offerings) are made.

Walking through the Old Town of my city, you'll see *ofrendas* consisting of everything from cigarettes and bottles of whiskey to Snickers candy bars and the traditional *pan de muerto* (sweet bread).

In Asian cultures, Tomb Sweeping Day is a time for families to clean an ancestor's tomb and pay respects to the dead person with offerings. The area around the tomb is cleaned and fresh soil is added. An ancestor's favorite food or drink will be left by the tomb, along with burning incense. If the family doesn't have access to the tomb, the same honoring ritual can be done at a home altar with offering a favorite food and saying prayers.

Cleaning the area around a grave is not limited to Asian cultures. While visiting a tiny cemetery in the Midwest where my great-grandmother is buried, my sister pulled all the weeds covering the flat tombstone, making sure the stone and the area surrounding it were clean and neat.

In Botswana, in Southern Africa, the ancestors provide the living with answers to everyday problems. People want to keep the ancestors happy to continue receiving their help and protection. This may take the form of prayers or sacrifices to the ancestors. The ancestors play a major role in the family: not only can they protect and bless; they can also curse and punish if their advice is not heeded. Curses can be either permanent or temporary, removed only by ritual. But the ancestors also bless, giving fertility to women and bringing needed rain during the correct growing season.

If you were raised in the Catholic faith, you'll know that the ancestors are honored on November 2, All Souls' Day. This is the day that commemorates the faithful departed, with names of those who died during the previous year read at Mass.

In America, military graves are decorated on Memorial Day as a way of honoring the service of military veterans. Originally known as Decoration Day, it's celebrated on the last Monday in May.

Honoring ancestors with food or drink isn't exclusive to one culture. In your own home, you may believe in serving up a tiny bite of food for the ancestors, or you may be one who pours a cup of coffee placed at an empty spot at the table to honor those who came before you. If you want to start your own tradition, draw a card and ask the ancestors in what way they want to be remembered.

As with all traditions, I'm a believer in doing what feels right for you. While I don't pour coffee in my mother's tiny Irish cup for her, I do put a pendulum in the cup that I want to use for ancestral work, asking for her blessing.

Tarot and Crystal Grids

I like to create crystal grids for ancestor work using tarot and the polished stones that I feel are right for the grid. If you've never worked with a crystal grid, there are several books that explore them in depth, among them *Crystal Gridwork* (Weiser Books, 2018) by Kiera Fogg.

First, understand that crystals carry Earth energy as well as the energy of your intention. Crystal grids can be created to manifest just about anything, but for now let's focus on creating one for your ancestral work.

A crystal grid is an actual formation designed almost like a tarot spread. Formations can vary from circles to pyramids to pentagrams or more. The crystals used are most often ones that correspond with whatever it is you want to work with.

For the grid you're going to create, ask the ancestors for help in the design. The pattern you create is going to be a personal one, based on your intent for directing the grid's energy.

When a crystal grid is being laid out and combined with your intention, you're engaging in sacred work, bringing together not only the vibrations and energy of the crystals but also the energy of you and your will. I see crystal grids as the sacred version of the electrical grids that power our cities and towns—except instead of powering a city, your crystal grid is powering your intention.

If I were an expert in sacred geometry, I'm sure I could explain to you in great detail how the grids' geometric shapes are little powerhouses on their own. Instead, I'm just going to leave it at saying that I have experienced their power and believe in their magic.

If you've worked with a tarot deck long enough, you know that there's an energy that's almost palpable. This isn't to say that the paper and its printed image hold some magical power, but rather that your energy imbued into the cards over time is magical. Combine tarot magic with crystal magic and your grids will be amazingly energetic.

How to Build Your Tarot Crystal Grid

First, set an intention. What do you want for your ancestral grid? To honor all the ancestors, one ancestor, for help clearing a pattern, or for healing? One other thing to consider is building a grid that honors something an ancestor held dear. For example, if the ancestor truly loved the mountains, think about how you can incorporate mountains in your grid. This could be something you manifest with a certain type of crystal or the shape you choose.

Another approach is to build a grid dedicated to a family unit's healing. I know if your family experience was a tough one, this might be a difficult grid to build. How can you put it together as a healing experience? It could be with the stones chosen, the shape, or a healing tarot card as the central core of the grid, e.g., the Queen of Cups.

Whatever your intention, make sure it's clear and you're focused on it while constructing your grid. If you're unsure of the difference between an intention and a goal, an *intention* is an authentic commitment that originates in your heart. For me, a *goal*, by contrast, is in your head. This is a sacred thing that you are committing to.

Next, pull a tarot card with the intention that the card's energy boosts the energy of the grid. Either randomly select a card or choose one from a faceup deck. Since you'll want to leave the card as part of the grid for some period of time, you may want to scan and print a copy of the card or draw a representation of it onto a blank card or index card in lieu of taking a card out of your deck.

Now, choose a focus stone. There are many websites that associate crystals with tarot cards. You can rely on one of those, or you can visit a local crystal shop and pick your focus stone. Once that stone is chosen, you're going to place it on top of the tarot card you picked.

Now the fun part begins: Decide on a shape for your grid. You can Google crystal grid shapes, but I prefer creating my own. Once the shape is in your mind, decide which crystals or polished stones to use to build the shape.

To give you a perspective on how all this comes together, let me stop here a sec and explain to you what I created and my thinking behind it.

I wanted a crystal grid with the intention of asking all my ancestors to help me in working to rebalance the planet. I randomly drew a card and up popped the Nine of Cups, often called the Wish card. A nice start.

I chose an aventurine as my focus stone for no other reason than I wanted a green stone, although it also helps that this stone is associated with abundance and harmony. The shape I decided on for my grid was a spiral, as spirals are found throughout nature and our own little Milky Way Galaxy is a spiral galaxy. Also, just personally, some of the most spiritual experiences of my life have been in walking a spiral labyrinth.

To build the spiral part of the grid, I picked out an assortment of polished stones, including lapis, jasper, sodalite, agate, carnelian, amethyst, quartz, rose quartz, and hematite. Because my intent was to ask the ancestors for help with Earth healing, I wanted a variety of the Earth's stones.

My crystal grid is shown on page 180.

What Are Tarot Gemstones?

Assuming you want to build your own ancestral crystal grid, you may want to use gemstones that correspond to tarot cards, particularly those of the Major Arcana. If you Google "tarot-gemstone correlation," you'll find lots of information online. Sometimes the info on different sites agrees, sometimes not. So how do you decide what crystals you may want to use to represent a Major Arcana for the ancestor with whom you're working?

I'm all in favor of using online sources and the many crystal books on the market describing the different energies of stones; however, I work more intuitively. What crystal I associate with the Emperor, for example, may have zip to do with what's commonly accepted. That's okay with me, because I'm the one the stone needs to energetically relate to.

Here's my own Major Arcana Crystal Correspondence chart. Feel free to use it, or one you found online, or one you create for yourself.

Tarot Card	Crystal
Fool	Azurite
Magician	Celestite
High Priestess	Moonstone
Empress	Aventurine
Emperor	Bloodstone
Hierophant	Apache tear
Lovers	Opal
Chariot	Jasper
Strength	Garnet
Hermit	Turquoise
Wheel of Fortune	Onyx
Justice	Lapis lazuli
Hanged Man	Sugilite
Death	Amber
Temperance	Amazonite
Devil	Chalcedony
Tower	Tourmaline
Star	Amethyst
Moon	Aquamarine
Sun	Citrine
Judgement	Rose quartz
World	Chrysocolla

TAROT ANCESTRAL CARDS

You know how, back in the day, men would pull out their wallet and show off their kids' pictures? Okay, maybe they still do that, but in my family, it's not a thing. You have to ask yourself—over time, what energy built up between the wallet carrier and the kids through having the kids' photo on the person's body all the time. Makes you wonder, doesn't it?

I'm not going to carry an ancestor's photo in my pocket or my wallet or even my handbag, but I do like having them around when doing my ancestral work. A long time ago I started creating ancestral cards, using printed scans of an ancestor's photo pasted on a blank card or index card. I know you may not have any pictures of your ancestors. In fact, I complain that my branch of the family didn't end up with any family photos, although we do have a few.

For this exercise you're going to make an ancestral card and set it where you can see it while you're working with family patterns, one of the tarot spreads in this book, or your crystal grid.

I wanted to work with my paternal grandfather and my maternal great-grandmother. Gramps passed over when I was one year old, so the only things I know about him are what I was told by other family members. Grandpa was a salesman who apparently liked wearing a big, flashy, fake diamond ring and playing the dandy. Unfortunately, he was held up at gunpoint once due to that big fake ring. He smoked all the time, loved chipped beef on toast, and was one helluva flashy dresser. It's no wonder that I drew the King of Wands for him.

To make Gramps's ancestral card, I scanned and printed a photo of him, pasted it onto a blank card, then added an image of a diamond and a cigarette. (I couldn't bring myself to look for a chipped beef on toast photo.) Now when I'm working with him I keep that card nearby as well as the King of Wands I drew for him earlier—mostly just to understand who he was. Together they evoke an energy that I love working with.

My great-grandmother passed over when she was thirty-three. The little I ever heard about her was that she was a kind woman whose death happened shortly after the loss of her young child. I've seen a photo of her, and all I can say is that she looks sweet and a little on the shy side. The ancestral card I created for her was a photo of her family along with a small insert of her tombstone.

If you choose to make cards for specific ancestors, I suggest keeping them out, either on an altar or wherever you do your ancestral work. I like being able to see the card at the same time I'm working with that specific person. I've also placed a card as the center of a crystal grid or made it the focus of an altar.

JOURNAL PROMPTS

1. The type of ritual I feel most drawn to is _____ .

That's because _____

_____ .

2. The items I've chosen for my ancestral altar are

_____ .

I picked these things because _____

_____ .

3. An ancestral practice from my country of origin is _____ .

I intend to incorporate this in my own ancestral practice by

_____

_____ .

Final Thoughts

Remember the very first spread you did in this book? It's time to go back and see how closely your experiences have mirrored the cards you drew. Was the outcome as expected or were there surprises along the way?

If you began Ancestral Tarot with the goal of healing old wounds, I hope your journey has been successful. If you simply wanted to give thanks for those who came before, may you feel their blessings.

My own journey has been an emotional one. It's brought an acceptance for things I can't change, gratitude for understanding old patterns, and some sadness for those family and friends I will always miss.

Thank you for joining me and our seventy-eight companions along the way. I wish you love and healing.

Appendix A: Tarot 101

TAROT STRUCTURE

Okay, let's just get this out of the way: Yes, there are a lot of cards in a deck, seventy-eight to be exact. And yes, it can take a long time to remember all of them—and even longer to be comfortable with interpreting the cards the way you want. But stick with me and I'll show you how to put all these puzzle pieces together in a way that makes sense.

THE SUITS

A tarot deck has seventy-eight cards; twenty-two are Major Arcana (numbered 0 21). These are all about big life themes. There are sixteen Court cards. These show personalities or personality traits. That leaves forty Minor Arcana (numbered Ace 10). These are all about everyday life. Below you'll find an explanation of why some cards are referred to as Minors and others are Majors.

The Minors and Courts are divided evenly between four suits (fourteen to each suit):

Cups—emotional stuff

Swords—mental stuff

Pentacles—physical stuff

Wands—passion stuff

As you can see, each suit has its own realm of influence.

If you know absolutely nothing more about tarot than this, you now know that if you draw a Cup card it's going to be dealing with emotions, while a Sword card is all about something in the mental realm. Keep this tidbit in mind as you move forward.

THE MINORS

Within each suit are cards numbered from 1 (Ace) to 10. They represent the everyday stuff of life: friendships, a crummy boss, relationship problems, money—all the things everyone deals with. Each number, regardless of suit, has a meaning.

You'll find zillions of tarot books that detail what each number means, but at their most basic, they are:

Ace—individual, me, first, new, pioneer

Two—relationships, diplomacy, duality, differing paths

Three—ease, celebration, joy, memory

Four—structure, foundation, stability, visionary

Five—change, loss, combativeness, competition, resignation

Six—harmony, calm, peace, kindness

Seven—beliefs, ethics, opportunity, spirituality

Eight—will, destiny, perfection, self-realization

Nine—principle, expectation, humanitarianism

Ten—completion, endings, realizations

Now that you know the numbers and the suits, you can weave them together. So if you pull a Five (change) of Swords (thoughts), the card is going have something to do with a change of ideas or thoughts. Likewise, an Ace (new) of Cups (emotion) indicates the beginning of something emotional.

Now here's the kicker: If you know that an Ace represents something new and Cups represent an emotion, how do you know *what* emotion? Here's where your intuition comes into play—and it's easier than you think. All you have to do is look at the card and lean into the impressions you get from what is pictured.

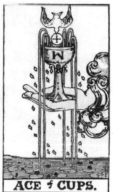

ACE ʄ CUPS.

What kind of emotion does this card look like it represents? Definitely not anger, frustration, tiredness, or any of a host of negative emotions. It's beautiful—water is overflowing from the cup, and the dove is dropping some kind of wafer into it. The cup and bird and hand are all posed above a sea of lily pads. What do *you* think the emotion is here? It could be love, could be gratitude, could be forgiveness.

And this is where my reading style differs from a traditional tarot book. What I see in a card and how it makes me feel are going to add a layer to whatever the book says.

Reading the Minors

If you know anything about astrology, you know that an astrological chart begins by placing a planet into a sign and into a house, e.g., Mars (planet) in Cancer (sign) in the fourth house.

Tarot works about the same. You're putting a number (or a Court) into a suit and coming up with an interpretation. This is a basic approach. The Five of Cups as an example: Five shows change. Cups show emotion. Would you interpret this as a change in heart? There's way more symbolism about this card—and all cards for that matter—but if you're just learning, getting these basics down will give you a foundation on which to add those further layers.

Once you have a general understanding of numbers and suits, now the fun comes in. Next, *look at the card.* The picture is going to add a third dimension to your knowledge.

Check out the Six of Swords. You know that Sixes are about harmony and Swords are about mental stuff. That in itself would tell you that the card is about harmonious thoughts.

But what happens when you explore the symbolism of the card? On one side of the boat the water is turbulent, on the other it's calm. How does this third dimension add to your understanding? Yep, it tells you that the person in the boat is leaving behind turbulent thoughts and moving into a period of more harmonious, calmer thinking.

Got it?

In a nutshell, that's the easiest way to read the Minors.

THE COURTS

The Court cards are the equivalent of the Jack, Queen, and King in playing cards, but with one additional card known as the Page, which, depending on deck used, may be called the Princess instead. Traditionally, the Courts represented people, identified by physical traits—eye color, gender, hair color, and so forth—as well as levels of age and maturity.

While Courts can represent a real person, I believe it's much more useful to think of them as personalities. They are:

Page—the kid who is an enthusiastic learner

Knight—the adventurer who is out on a quest, and sometimes overly excitable

Queen—the feminine expression of her suit (e.g., the Queen of Pentacles will feed you while the Queen of Cups will dry your tears)

King—the mature manifestation of his suit

Combining Courts with suits, you know that the Knight of Cups is searching for some emotion (typically love) while the Knight of Swords is on an intellectual quest (think about a young man learning to be a chess master). This particular Knight of Swords looks like the kind of guy who would rush into something without a single thought—and yet he's the Knight of Thoughts.

KNIGHT of SWORDS.

For me, this Knight looks like he's deliriously happy rushing in to learn something new. In fact, he's my favorite of all the Knights, maybe because I rush in where I sometimes shouldn't!

If the Courts give you the willies when it comes to interpreting them, use the Courts' chart (see page 190) and associate each of the sixteen Courts with someone you know *based on their astrological sign*. Or assign a Court to sixteen people you know based on their personality.

You'll find this exercise helpful once you start drawing Court cards to represent an ancestor's personality. This also works for finding the card that represents you!

Here's an example that might help you with the Courts: Charles, Prince of Wales, is a Scorpio, so his tarot card is the Knight of Cups. You know from earlier that the Knight's quest and Cups are about emotions. This tells us that, at his core, he seeks the things that feed his emotional body.

Diana, Princess of Wales, was a Cancer, giving her the Queen of Cups. This Queen is the embodiment of her suit (Cups). This means, at her core, she had a great desire—a need actually—to envelop the world in love. (If you're into astrology, you'll also note that Cancers are the moms of the zodiac.) She would have wanted to hug you and make you feel emotionally secure. She would feel comfortable holding the world in her arms, while the Knight (Charles) would have flitted from one quest to the next.

Court Card	Keywords	Astrological Correspondence
Page of Pentacles	Learning how to manifest, voracious learner, responsible	Capricorn
Knight of Pentacles	Slow moving, conservative, methodical	Taurus
Queen of Pentacles	Physically nurturing, motherly, secure home	Capricorn
King of Pentacles	Successful, disciplined, financially secure	Virgo
Page of Swords	Curious, easily distractable, quick-witted	Gemini
Knight of Swords	Energetic, unstoppable, restless	Aquarius
Queen of Swords	Intelligent, independent, truth-speaker	Libra
King of Swords	Intellectual, detached, professional	Gemini
Page of Wands	Free spirit, creative, active	Aries
Knight of Wands	Passionate, impulsive, seeking action	Leo
Queen of Wands	Determined, bold, friendly	Aries
King of Wands	Visionary, gets things done, leader	Sagittarius
Page of Cups	Beginning of a creative project, intuitive, emotional	Cancer
Knight of Cups	Charming, questing for love, exploring passions	Scorpio
Queen of Cups	Intuitive, compassionate, emotionally nurturing	Cancer
King of Cups	Emotionally balanced, kind, supportive	Pisces

If working with celebs helps you understand the Courts, go for it. Jay-Z (Sagittarius) and Beyoncé (Virgo), perhaps?

THE MAJORS

Lastly, tarot has twenty-two Major Arcana cards, shown in the table on page 192. Majors represents the big themes of our existence, the archetypal energies that include life, death, resurrection, knowledge, and justice. The Majors are numbered 0–21.

In the Major cheat sheet, I've included astrological signs, planets, and keywords. The more layers you can add to the Majors, the better you'll be at interpreting them.

Take, for example, the Justice card. On the surface she looks like balance, which is one of her keywords. But if you dig into the symbolism—and this is where I encourage you to pick up a basic tarot book—her double-edged sword represents what is correct/logical, the law. She is not blindfolded, meaning she sees everything clearly.

Her scales show us the result of cause and effect and karma. Did you smoke three packs of cigarettes for ten years (cause)? If so, a lung disease (effect) is probably going to tip those scales out of balance. Justice metes out the reward or punishment.

I know it's a lot to take in, so if you run into problems down the line as you work through this book, come back here and use the cheat sheet or other tools to help you interpret the cards you're pulling.

Want to try one more? How about the Hierophant (known as the Pope in some decks)?

This card has too much symbolism to cover in depth, but guiding you back to the cheat sheet, you can see that the astrological sign associated

	Tarot	Sign/Planet	Element	Keywords
0	Fool	Uranus	Air	Innocence, trust
1	Magician	Mercury	Air	Manifestation
2	High Priestess	Moon	Water	Inner knowing
3	Empress	Venus	Earth	Creativity
4	Emperor	Aries	Fire	Foundations
5	Hierophant	Taurus	Earth	Teachings
6	Lovers	Gemini	Air	Relationships
7	Chariot	Cancer	Water	Movement
8	Strength	Leo	Fire	Mind over matter
9	Hermit	Virgo	Earth	Reflection
10	Wheel of Fortune	Jupiter	Fire	Chance
11	Justice	Libra	Air	Balance
12	Hanged Man	Neptune	Water	Stillness
13	Death	Scorpio	Water	Change
14	Temperance	Sagittarius	Fire	Blending
15	Devil	Capricorn	Earth	Addiction
16	Tower	Mars	Fire	Destruction
17	Star	Aquarius	Air	Hope
18	Moon	Pisces	Water	Hidden
19	Sun	Sun	Fire	Brilliant
20	Judgement	Pluto	Fire	New life
21	The World	Saturn	Earth	Completion

with the Hierophant is Taurus. This religious figure teaches us how to live within our own belief structure. If your religion is dogmatic, he will show you how to maintain the dogma. To that end, he can be inflexible and unyielding. If you've ever known a Taurus, I'm pretty sure you can relate. At his core, though, he is the teacher, guiding us on a level path that flows between heaven and Earth. Want to learn how to live an Earth-centric life? He can teach you, but you better remember that he's not too crazy about you leaving the path you asked to walk.

When you begin working with the ancestors, you'll be using Minors to understand their everyday life, Courts to understand personality, and Majors to understand the major themes of their life and times. It's important that you make this distinction between the three entities while at the same time learn to weave them together into a comprehensive whole.

Appendix B: Tarot Practice Resources

Recommended Reading

Astrology for Real Life: A Workbook for Beginners by Theresa Reed (Weiser Books, 2019).

Best Tarot Practices: Everything You Need to Know to Learn the Tarot by Marcia Masino (Weiser Books, 2009).

Beyond the Celtic Cross: Secret Techniques for Taking Tarot to an Exciting New Level by Paul Hughes-Barlow and Catherine Chapman (Aeon Books, 2009).

Germanic Magic: Runes: Their History, Mythology, and Use in Modern Magical Practice by Gunivortus Goos (Books on Demand, 2019).

Holistic Tarot: An Integrative Approach to Using Tarot for Personal Growth by Benebell Wen (North Atlantic Books, 2015).

Jung and Tarot: An Archetypal Journey by Sallie Nichols (Samuel Weiser, 2004).

Kitchen Table Tarot by Melissa Cynova (Llewellyn Publications, 2017).

Mary K. Greer's 21 Ways to Read a Tarot Card by Mary Greer (Llewellyn Publications, 2011).

Nordic Runes: Understanding, Casting, and Interpreting the Ancient Viking Oracle by Paul Rhys Mountfort (Destiny Books, 2003).

Seventy-Eight Degrees of Wisdom: A Tarot Journey to Self-Awareness by Rachel Pollack (Weiser Books, 2019).

Spiritual Protection: A Safety Manual for Energy Workers, Healers, and Psychics by Sophie Reicher (Weiser Books, 2010).

Taking Up the Runes: A Complete Guide to Using Runes in Spells, Rituals, Divination, and Magic by Diana L. Paxson (Weiser Books, 2005).

Tarot: No Questions Asked: Mastering the Art of Intuitive Reading by Theresa Reed (Weiser Books, 2020).

The Tarot: A Key to the Wisdom of the Ages by Paul Foster Case (Tarcher/ Perigee, 2006).

Tarot and Astrology: Enhance Your Readings with the Wisdom of the Zodiac by Corrine Kenner (Llewellyn Publications, 2012).

The Tarot Coloring Book by Theresa Reed (Sounds True, 2016).

Tarot Elements: Five Readings to Reset Your Life by Melissa Cynova (Llewellyn Publications, 2019).

Tarot for Troubled Times by Theresa Reed and Shaheen Miro (Weiser Books, 2019).

The Tarot Handbook: Practical Applications of Ancient Visual Symbols by Angeles Arrien (Jeremy P. Tarcher/Putnam, 1997).

Tarot Inspired Life: Use the Cards to Enhance Your Life by Jaymi Elford (Llewellyn Publications, 2019).

Tarot 101: Mastering the Art of Reading the Cards by Kim Huggens (Llewellyn Publications, 2010).

Tarot Plain and Simple by Anthony Louis (Llewellyn Publications, 2010).

365 Tarot Spreads: Revealing the Magic in Each Day by Sasha Graham (Llewellyn Publications, 2014).

Who Are You in the Tarot? Discover Your Birth and Year Cards and Uncover Your Destiny by Mary K. Greer (Weiser Books, 2011).

Apps

I will often purchase a tarot app for a deck I already own if I want to examine the symbols more closely. The apps in this list are only suggestions, based on my personal preference. If you're not sure which app or which deck to purchase, the Fool's Dog Tarot Sampler (free) has samples of sixty different decks. Download it to get a flavor of decks you may want.

Astro Gold (astrology)

Chrysalis Tarot

Deluxe Moon

Druid Oracles

DruidCraft Tarot

Fairy Tale Lenormand

The Fool's Dog Tarot Sampler (free)

Golden Thread Tarot (free)

Housewives Tarot

Luminous Spirit Tarot (free)

Mystic Mondays Tarot (free)

Mystical Cats Tarot

Robin Wood Tarot

Rocketbook Digital Journal and app

Tarot Mucha

Wildwood Tarot

Wizards Tarot

Appendix C: Genealogy Resources

FREE RESOURCES

Has ancestral work given you an itch to learn more about your ancestors? If so, here are my favorite free websites.

AfriGeneas

www.afrigeneas.com

This site is dedicated to African American genealogy research. For best results, start with the Beginner's Guide, which is listed under the Records tab. From there, search the slave, marriage, death, and surname databases. The site also has an active user forum and mailing list.

Ancestry

ancestry.com

This is not a free site, but here's a tricky way to get value from it if you've done one of the *Ancestry.com* DNA tests. Once logged into your account, which you get with your DNA test, use the Search link to do a search for someone in your ancestry. A list of possible records will come up, including census, military, death, and marriages. Make a note of those records, e.g., 1920 federal census, Iowa marriages, etc. Then, go over to the *FamilySearch.org* site and see if they have those records there. Here's the cool thing: FamilySearch has all the U.S. federal census records from 1790 through 1940, and they're all free.

Civil War Soldiers and Sailors Database

www.nps.gov

Using records from the National Archives and Records Administration (NARA), this database contains the names and information for over six million men who served in the Union and Confederate armed forces during the Civil War. Once you've found your ancestor in the database, you'll also learn his rank, battle unit (e.g., Third Regiment, Missouri Cavalry), function (infantry, cavalry, artillery), and name of ship for those in the navy. Often you'll also find a link to the regimental history, so you can see where your ancestor fought throughout the course of the war.

CyndisList

www.cyndislist.com

This site has been around for over twenty years and is a compilation of links to over 300,000 genealogy resources. This site has more than 200 categories, so be sure to browse them just to get a sense of what you can find here. Not only are there categories for places, such as states or countries, but also for things like funeral homes, podcasts, and scrapbooks. You never know what you can find, and it's one of those sites you can sit on for hours, just because the links will send you down a lot of rabbit holes.

FamilySearch

familysearch.org

This website, owned by the Church of Jesus Christ of Latter-Day Saints (LDS), has one of the largest online collections of free genealogy data. You'll have to sign up for an account, but that's free too. Once on the site, you can search several different databases, including books that have been digitized. If you're lucky, someone will have already written a book about your family or mentioned them in a history or family tree book. Because there are so many user-generated trees on the site, you also have the chance of finding family photos that a distant cousin has uploaded. One of the best things about this site, other than it being free, is that its records are worldwide, not just U.S.-based.

FreeBMD

www.freebmd.org.uk

If your ancestors lived in England or Wales, you're going to love this site. It's a volunteer effort to transcribe the Civil Registration index of births, marriages, and deaths for the two. On the home page you'll see links to Free UK Genealogy, FreeCEN (census), and FreeREG (Parish Registers). In total, there are more than 357 million available records.

JewishGen

jewishgen.org

Doing Jewish research? This is a must-use site. You'll find both free tutorials great for the beginning researcher and paid classes. Databases include those for Jewish surnames, family trees, towns, Holocaust victims, and burials.

Library and Archives of Canada

www.bac-lac.gc.ca

Each database on this site has its own help section, so if you run into problems, be sure to check out the help sections. Some of the links here go to microfilm records, others to transcribed data that's online. You'll find a wide variety of records from birth and marriage certificates to land, census, and immigration records.

One-Step Webpages by Stephen P. Morse

stevemorse.org

While this site looks a little intimidating to find your way around in, it has useful information and links for immigration records. Included here are links to passenger list manifests, which list the names of individuals immigrating to America. Ports include New York, Baltimore, New Orleans, Philadelphia, San Francisco, and the Canadian ports of Quebec, Montreal, St. John, and Halifax.

The Proceedings of the Old Bailey, 1674-1913

www.oldbaileyonline.org

Okay, just for a little fun. If your ancestor might have been on the wrong side of the law, and lived in London, he might have shown up in this database of criminals brought before the Old Bailey, the Central Criminal Court in London. It's kind of a shocker to see how severe the punishments were for benign crimes, including death, burning the hand, branding, and being sent to America for seven years of indentured servitude.

USGenWeb

usgenweb.org

For those just getting started in American genealogy, this is a great first stop. The site is run by volunteers and organized by state and then county. If you know which county your family lived in, click over to see available resources. Some county admins have loaded up their portion of the site with a search engine and cemetery, military, marriage, death, and historical records. Other admins are a bit less ambitious. You don't have to sign up to use the site. Just go to the link, choose your state, and then county to begin searching.

WorldGenWeb

worldgenweb.org

The worldwide version of the USGenWeb is organized by country and then some by political divisions of county or province. The most common links you'll find on the site are to Facebook groups, Wikipedia entries, message boards, genealogy societies, and maps.

LOCAL GENEALOGY SOCIETIES

If there's a genealogy society where your ancestor lived, contact them. Not only do they have interesting records, they often have personal knowledge of a family who lived in their town generations ago. Additionally, I've never found one where the people weren't happy to help in my search.

TEN STEPS TO GETTING STARTED IN CLIMBING YOUR FAMILY TREE

1. Start with yourself and work backward, not the other way around.

2. Talk to your oldest living relatives. Once they're gone, so is their firsthand knowledge.

3. Document your family data in a free genealogy software program (see below).

4. Get help from your local genealogy society—almost every town has one.

5. Search free records online.

6. Visit your local family history library if your town has one. Ask for help—they'll get you started.

7. Contact the cousins, tell them what you're doing, and ask for their memories along with copies of photos and documents they might have.

8. Pick a project. For example, once you find your first nineteenth-century ancestor, learn all you can about them before going off to look for someone else.

9. Record where you find everything. Trust me, you'll kick yourself if you don't do this one.

10. Check *FamilySearch.org* for digitized books. See if a book about the family has already been written.

Free Genealogy Software

My two favorite genealogy software programs are

LegacyFamilyTree—*legacyfamilytree.com*

RootsMagic—*rootsmagic.com*

Both programs have paid versions with a few more bells and whistles, but the free versions are all you'll need. These are free to download and easy to use.

About the Author

NANCY HENDRICKSON is an author with decades of experience in genealogy and tarot. Among her published works are several genealogy books including the *Unofficial Guide to Ancestry.com* and several magazine articles. Nancy has been interviewed on the topic of internet genealogy by the *New York Times*, *Kiplinger's*, and *Better Homes and Gardens*. She is a columnist for *The Cartomancer Magazine*, writing about tarot decks of the past as well as tarot from a cultural perspective. She posts daily about tarot and other forms of divination on Instagram (*@nancysageshadow*). Learn more about Nancy at *www.sageandshadow.com*.

To Our Readers

Weiser Books, an imprint of Red Wheel/Weiser, publishes books across the entire spectrum of occult, esoteric, speculative, and New Age subjects. Our mission is to publish quality books that will make a difference in people's lives without advocating any one particular path or field of study. We value the integrity, originality, and depth of knowledge of our authors.

Our readers are our most important resource, and we appreciate your input, suggestions, and ideas about what you would like to see published.

Visit our website at *www.redwheelweiser.com* to learn about our upcoming books and free downloads, and be sure to go to *www.redwheelweiser.com/newsletter* to sign up for newsletters and exclusive offers.

You can also contact us at *info@rwwbooks.com* or at

Red Wheel/Weiser, LLC
65 Parker Street, Suite 7
Newburyport, MA 01950